"*George Orwell: Life, Writing, and the Making of a Political Conscience* makes a boon companion for both first-time visitors and returning travelers to the singular land of Orwell. Steven Schlesser has a gift for the granular that meshes nicely with his subject's talent for vivid detail. This compact and readable book capably primes the reader for an initial pass at, or a subsequent brush-up on, some of the finest writing in the English language."

—Gary D. Cole, author of *Artless*

"An insightful and impactful summary of the sociological and political influences underpinning Orwell's major works. In particular, Schlesser shows us how Orwell had to live among the underclass before writing so poignantly about them."

—Jim McDermott, author of *Bitter Is The Wind*

"George Orwell was one of the most important writers of the twentieth century and is still essential reading if we want to understand how we got to where we are today. His *Animal Farm* and *Nineteen Eighty-Four* are still best-sellers. If all the books in print today were destroyed except for twenty, his *Nineteen Eighty-Four* would be a priority to save among the others.

That is why it is such a pleasure to see Steven Schlesser summarize Orwell's life and writings once again. We can never have enough of George Orwell. He was the conscience of the twentieth century in the West, and volunteered to fight against fascism in the Spanish Civil War in 1936, blithely saying, 'The rise in fascism – somebody's got to put a stop to it.'"

—John Harte, author of *The Passionate Spies*

# GEORGE ORWELL

## Life, Writing, and the Making of a Political Conscience

**STEVEN SCHLESSER**

All he can say is, 'Behave decently,' which, as I suggested earlier, is not necessarily so shallow as it sounds.

—George Orwell from his essay 'Charles Dickens.'

George Orwell: Life, Writing, and the Making of a Political Conscience
by Steven Schlesser

Cune Press, Seattle 2026

| | |
|---|---|
| Paperback | ISBN 9781951082994 |
| EPUB | ISBN 9781614572909 |

Library of Congress Cataloging-in-Publication Data

Names: Schlesser, Steven, 1957- author
Title: George Orwell : life, writing, and the making of a political conscience / Steven Schlesser.
Description: Seattle : Cune Press, 2026. | Includes bibliographical references.
Identifiers: LCCN 2026009949 (print) | LCCN 2026009950 (ebook) | ISBN 9781951082994 trade paperback | ISBN 9781614572909 epub
Subjects: LCSH: Orwell, George, 1903-1950 | Authors, English--20th century | English literature--20th century--History and criticism | LCGFT: Biographies
Classification: LCC PR6029.R8 Z7814 2026 (print) | LCC PR6029.R8 (ebook)
LC record available at https://lccn.loc.gov/2026009949
LC ebook record available at https://lccn.loc.gov/2026009950

Cune Press: www.cunepress.com | www.salaamculturalmuseum.org

This book is dedicated to the memory of
Brewster Wilson, 1921-1957,
assassinated in the service of his country in Iran.

# Author's Note

It took me two years to write this short book on George Orwell. Of course I've been studying him for decades. The process for writing this was helped tremendously by having my daughter, Lucy Schlesser, organize the material. Each weekend I would send her the appropriate text and then, during the following week, I would think about what I would send next. Also I think it is important to mention the value of audio books in our busy, distracted age. The narrator for most books on Orwell is Frederick Davidson, also known as David Case. Sadly he has passed away, but his perfect British voice remains.

stevenschlesser@gmail.com

# Table of Contents

Preface 13

Chapter 1: School Days 14

Chapter 2: Burma 23

Chapter 3: Paris and London 30

Chapter 4: Wigan Pier 45

Chapter 5: Spain 54

Chapter 6: World War Two 62

Chapter 7: Animal Farm 69

Chapter 8: 1984 76

Bibliography 97

Suggested Further Reading 98

About Cune Press 100

Books from Cune Press 101

About the Author 102

# Preface

I WROTE THIS BOOK TO ACQUAINT READERS, particularly students, with the life and works of George Orwell. Scholars ahead of me have written lengthy, well-researched biographies, but I wanted to keep this book short and accessible, using Orwell's words as much as possible, and to focus on his most important works in terms of his development as a writer and political thinker.

To keep the presentation simple, I used only one outside source—that is, Bernard Crick's early biography of Orwell (Penguin, 1980). For the rest I turned to Orwell's own writing, particularly the material found in these books, *Down and Out in Paris and London*, *The Road to Wigan Pier*, *Homage to Catalonia*, *Animal Farm*, and *1984*. I also drew from the four volume *Collected Essays Journalism and Letters of George Orwell* that was assembled by his widow, Sonia Orwell (Harcourt Brace Jovanovich, 1974). Attributions appear in the text.

Producing this little book was a process of selection. Nevertheless, getting the word out on Orwell—even if much is left out—is more important than ever given that he is the most often referenced English speaking writer in modern times.

# School Days

George Orwell was the middle child, and only son, of parents who both had colonial connections. His father, Richard Blair, had descended from clergy as well as from a Scottish slave-owner of tropical plantations in Jamaica. His mother, Ida Mabel Limouzin, came from a French family of teak merchants who had made money, ironically, in Burma. By the time Ida and Richard married both family fortunes had disappeared.

Perhaps it is rather fitting that the author of whom we think as quintessentially English was French on his mother's side and Scottish on his father's side. Orwell had a happy childhood. Raised on the southern English coast, Orwell had two sisters, one older and one younger, each separated from her brother by five years. His mother, an energetic woman, doted on him. For the most part his father remained away from the family, stationed in India as a sub-inspector in the British colonial service that oversaw the export of opium to China from India. Richard Blair performed his duties with a methodical dullness and without any moral reservations whatsoever.

Orwell was born in India in 1903, christened Eric Arthur Blair. A year after his birth, his mother took the opportunity to take the two children back to England for schooling and to set a pattern for the family in which the gruff, dull, unimaginative father would stay in India, and the attractive, vivacious mother would remain with the children in England. During those rare visits when his father came home, Orwell remembered him:

"I merely disliked my father, whom I had barely seen before I was eight and who appeared to me simply as a gruff-voiced elderly man forever saying, 'Don't.'" CEJL Vol. 4, p. 360.

Orwell's parents did not have a soul-mate marriage, but as so often happened in England before WWI, they made do. When Orwell's father retired and returned to England, he and Orwell's mother maintained separate bedrooms and separate interests, even attending separate bridge parties. Looking back, Orwell rarely mentioned family issues or problems in the marriage. Instead, he chronicled his own interior life and his literary development:

"From a very early age, perhaps the age of five or six, I knew that when I grew up, I should be a writer. Between the ages of about seventeen and twenty-four I tried to abandon this idea, but I did so with the consciousness that I was outraging my true nature and that sooner or later I should have to settle down and write books. I was the middle child of three, but there was a gap of five years on either side, and I barely saw my father before I was eight. For this and other reasons I was somewhat lonely, and I soon developed disagreeable mannerisms which made me unpopular throughout my school days. I had the lonely child's habit of making up stories and holding conversations with imaginary persons, and I think from the very start my literary ambitions were mixed up with the feeling of being isolated and undervalued." CEJL Vol. 1, p.1.

That feeling of being isolated and undervalued would stay with him throughout his next step which was being sent at eight to a preparatory school called St. Cyprian's. As the son of a colonial civil servant, Orwell was expected to follow the path of higher education—not so much Oxford or Cambridge but rather Eton, Harrow, Rugby or other 'public' schools. This kind of education was a mark of status and would propel a young man forward as a symbol of status into the class-ridden British society. Entry into promising careers such as the Army, Church, and Civil Service as well as the professions depended on young men doing well 'at school.' Orwell's path was typical: St. Cyprian's, Eton, and then colonial civil service. Orwell, as we shall see, wrote scathingly about his preparatory school but he never would have been 'Orwell' had he not been forced to embark on this path.

St. Cyprian's was one of the newer preparatory schools, run by its headmaster and owner Vaughan Wilkes and his wife. The school was only twelve years old in 1911 when Orwell arrived there and already had a reputation for landing their students at Harrow and other prominent public schools. Mr. Wilkes sought to include scholarship students who showed promise to achieve entry into these schools. The fees were set at 180 pounds a year. Orwell, whose father was soon to retire on a pension of about 440 pounds a year, was taken on with a scholarship (his dues were half, a sum his parents could just afford) and throughout his time at St. Cyprian's he was reminded that he was attending almost by the grace of Mr. and Mrs. Wilkes.

Mr. Wilkes had two great ambitions. "One was to attract titled boys to the school, and the other was to train pupils to win scholarships at the public schools, above all Eton… . All the very rich boys were more or less undisguisedly favoured. The school still had a faint suggestion of the Victorian 'private academy' with its 'parlour borders' and when I later read about that kind of school in Thackeray immediately saw the resemblance. I doubt whether Sambo (Mr. Wilkes) ever caned any boy whose father's income was much above 2000 pounds a year. But he was sometimes willing to sacrifice financial profit to scholastic prestige. Occasionally, by special arrangement, he would take at greatly reduced fees some boy who seemed likely to win scholarships and thus bring credit on the school. It was on these terms that I was at St. Cyprian's myself: otherwise my parents could not have afforded to send me to such an expensive school." CEJL Vol. 4, p. 335-336.

Even though Orwell came to the school by special arrangement, he was more often reminded of his parents' relative poverty rather than of his own academic promise.

"I did not at first understand that I was being taken at reduced fees; it was only when I was about eleven that Flip and Sambo (Mr. and Mrs. Wilkes) began throwing that fact in my teeth. For the first two or three years I went through the ordinary educational mill: then, soon after I started Greek (one started Latin at eight, Greek at ten), I moved into the scholarship class, which was taught, so far as classics went, largely by Sambo himself. Over a period of two or three years the scholarship boys were crammed with learning as cynically as a goose is crammed for Christmas." CEJL Vol. 4, p. 336.

Looking back on it, Orwell recognized that this kind of education—cramming the mind of a twelve year old boy solely for the sake of an examination to win entry to a prestigious public school—was an evil thing at best and often ruined a gifted boy's career in its tracks. In addition, Mrs. Wilkes would regularly remind Orwell about his family's financial difficulties.

"Long before I grasped the nature of my financial relationship with Sambo, I had been made to understand that I was not on the same footing as most of the other boys… I never, for instance, succeeded in getting a cricket bat of my own because 'Your parents wouldn't be able to afford it'. This phrase pursued me throughout my school days. At St. Cyprian's we were not allowed to keep the money we brought back with us, but had to 'give it in' on the first day of term, and then from time to time were allowed to spend it under supervision. I and similarly-placed boys were always choked off from buying expensive toys like model airplanes, even if the necessary money stood to our credit. Flip, in particular, seemed to aim consciously at inculcating a humble outlook in the poorer boys. "Do you think that's the sort of thing a boy like you should buy?" I remember her saying to somebody—and she said this in front of the whole school: 'You know you're not going to grow up with money, don't you? Your people aren't rich. You must learn to be sensible. Don't get above yourself!'" CEJL Vol. 4, p. 339.

Flip and Sambo would further humiliate Orwell, not only by constantly zeroing in on the fact that his family was less well off than most of the other families but also discussing the same subject between them, as if the young Orwell was not in earshot.

"Flip would search me with her baleful eyes… 'I don't think it's awfully decent of you to behave like this, is it? Do you think it's quite playing the game by your mother and father to go on idling your time away, week after week, month after month? Do you *want* to throw all your chances away? You know your people aren't rich, don't you? You know they can't afford the same things as other boys' parents. How are they to send you to a public school if you don't win a scholarship? I know how proud your mother is of you. Do you *want* to let her down?"

"I don't think he wants to go to a public school any longer," Sambo would say, addressing himself to Flip with a pretense that I was not there. "I think he's given up that idea. He wants to be a little office boy at forty pounds a year." CEJL Vol. 4, p.341.

In painting these word portraits of his former headmaster and his wife, Orwell not only finds the telling details (and the perfect pitch of their dialogue) but presents these details with flair and originality. One of the signatures of Orwell's writing is what I call 'presenting the unusual and sordid details' with freshness and clarity. In fact, Orwell seemed to *relish* writing about these details. Many of those who graduated from St. Cyprian's (the famous golf commentator Henry Longhurst among them) remember all the good things—the morning bugle calls, the athletic events, the rigors of learning Latin and Greek. Not

Orwell. In his remarkable essay 'Such, Such Were the Joys' written thirty years after his time there, Orwell gives us the seamier side of the school:

"I do not want to claim that I was a martyr or that St. Cyprian's was a sort of Dotheboys Hall. But I should be falsifying my own memories if I did not record that they are largely memories of disgust. The overcrowded, underfed, underwashed life that we led *was* disgusting, as I recall it. If I shut my eyes and say 'school', it is of course the physical surroundings that first come back to me: the flat playing-field with its cricket pavilion and the little shed by the rifle range, the draughty dormitories, the dusty, splintery passages, the square of asphalt in front of the gymnasium, the raw-looking pinewood chapel at the back. And at almost every point some filthy detail protrudes itself. For example, there were the pewter bowls out of which we had porridge. They had overhanging rims, and under the rims there were accumulations of sour porridge, which could be flaked off in long strips. The porridge itself, too, contained more lumps, hairs and unexplained black things than one would have thought impossible, unless someone were putting them there on purpose. It was never safe to start on the porridge without investigating it first. And there was the slimy water of the plunge bath—it was twelve or fifteen feet long, the whole school was supposed to go into it every morning, and I doubt whether the water was changed at all frequently—and the always-damp towels with their cheesy smell: and, on occasional visits in the winter, the murky sea water of the local Baths, which came straight from the beach and on which I once saw floating a human turd. And the sweaty smell of the changing-room with its greasy basins, and, giving on this, the row of filthy, dilapidated lavatories, which had no fastenings of any kind on the doors, so that whenever you were sitting there someone was sure to come crashing in. It is not easy for me to think of my school days without seeming to breath in a whiff of something cold and evil-smelling—a sort of compound of sweaty stockings, dirty towels, faecal smells blowing along corridors, forks with old food between the prongs, neck-of-mutton stew, and the banging doors of the lavatories and the echoing chamber-pots in the dormitories." CEJL Vol. 4, p. 347-348.

Of course, within this paragraph are the characteristic Orwell touches: the porridge which "could be flaked off in long strips" and the human turd floating on the seawater. One imagines Orwell writing these lines with amusement and satisfaction as a rebuke to all those British public school boys who in later life glorified their own school days. Several graduates of St. Cyprian's said they owed their success and toughness to the training they received there. Henry Longhurst wrote in his autobiography that he had received a letter from a colleague: "It may amuse you to know that my brother attributes the fact that he emerged absolutely sane and fit from five years as a prisoner of war solely to having been at St. Cyprian's" Crick, p. 61.

The British novelist Evelyn Waugh said that the poorer boys who went to secondary school during the day, and could come home each evening to a warm, loving family, suffered terribly in prison whereas the public school boys who had been to preparatory schools "did just fine" being locked up.

Orwell titled his essay from a stanza in a William Blake poem (wonderful irony here too):

Such, such were the joys
  When we all, girls and boys,
In our youth time were seen,
  On the Echoing Green.
Crick, p. 66.

Well before he wrote this essay, Orwell took opportunities to comment on the follies of British preparatory schools. ('Such, Such Were the Joys' was written before 1947). In 1941, in reviewing a novel by Stephen Spender called *The Backward Son*, he wrote:

"It is about a 'prep school,' one of those (on the whole) nasty little schools at which small boys are prepared for the public school entrance examination. Incidentally these schools with their money-grubbing proprietors and their staff of underpaid hacks, are responsible for a lot of the harm that is usually to blame on the public schools. A majority of middle-class boys have their minds permanently lamed by them before they are thirteen years old." Crick, p. 67.

Various commentators have raised issues about Orwell over-exaggerating the negative aspects of his experience at St. Cyprian's especially given that he wrote the piece thirty years later and given that as a writer he had matured into looking at the 'underside' of society, and of course at his own experiences. Nevertheless, he was able to portray effectively the psychological impact on a child of being snatched away from home at a tender age and thrust into a hostile environment.

For the young Orwell, a by-product of the hostile environment of his new school was that he involuntarily wet his bed. This kind of thing happens to an eight-year-old. Orwell opens the essay with the subject of his nighttime bed wetting. He overhears Flip discussing his bed wetting with a woman who is visiting the school. The woman was dressed in riding clothes and seemed to Orwell quite masculine. Somehow Orwell got the impression that Flip had given this woman permission to beat him should he wet his bed again. He thought her name was "Mrs. Form" whereas Flip had said she would give permission to the Sixth Form (favored upperclassmen) to beat him if he again wet his bed. Sure enough, young Orwell wet his bed in the night without having known he had done so. Instead of being punished by the Sixth Form, the headmaster, Sambo, administered the blows with a riding crop. As he did so, he kept time with the blows by saying "you dir-ty lit-tle boy" repeatedly (a perfect Orwell detail). Looking back on this treatment, Orwell noted:

"I knew that bed-wetting was (a) wicked and (b) outside my control. The second fact I was personally aware of, and the first I did not question. It was possible, therefore, to commit a sin without knowing that you committed it, without wanting to commit it, and without being able to avoid it. Sin was not necessarily something that you did: it might be something that happened to you. I do not want to claim that this idea flashed into my mind as a complete novelty at this very moment, under the blows of Sambo's cane: I must have had glimpses of it before I left home, for my early childhood had not been altogether happy. But at any rate this was the one great abiding lesson of my boyhood: that I was in a world where it was *not possible* for me to be good." CEJL Vol. 4, p. 334.

Much of young Orwell's confusion arose from his ignorance of his status as a bright student. From his perspective, he was to be pitied because along with wetting his bed he came from a family that was not rich. What Orwell did not realize then was that he stood to win scholarships to those much-heralded public schools and thus bring prestige to Sambo and Flip and their school. In addition, there was a sort of a fawning obsequiousness in his attitude towards these two, a feeling also mingled with hatred:

"A child believes that the school exists to educate and that the schoolmaster disciplines him either for his own good, or from a love of bullying. Flip and Sambo had chosen to befriend me, and their friendship included canings, reproaches, and humiliations, which were good for me and which saved me from an office stool. That was their version, and I believed in it. It was therefore clear that I owed them a vast debt of gratitude. But I was *not* grateful as I very well knew. On the contrary, I hated both of them. I could not control my subjective feelings, and I could not conceal them from myself. But it is wicked, is it not, to hate your benefactors? So I was taught, and so I believed. A child accepts the codes of behavior that are presented to it, even when it breaks them." CEJL Vol. 4, p. 343.

Orwell's school days were coming to an end. Not only his time at St. Cyprian's but also his time at Wellington (of which he wrote very little) before attending Eton. It was the end of winter term when he left St. Cyprian's forever. "With a sense of coming out of darkness into sunlight I put on my Old Boy's tie as we dressed for the journey… .I was escaping from bondage… For years past I had been resolved—unconsciously at first, but consciously later on—that once my scholarship was won I would 'slack off' and cram no longer. This resolve, by the way, was so fully carried out that between the ages of thirteen and twenty-two or three I hardly ever did a stroke of avoidable work." CEJL Vol. 4, p. 363.

Orwell kept to his resolve. He did not make much of an impression during his time at Eton, and Eton did not make much impression on him:

"I had been lucky enough to win a scholarship, but I did not work there and learned very little, and I don't feel that Eton has been much of a formative influence in my life." Crick, p. 100. There were, however, several aspects of the school he complimented. The atmosphere of the school, he wrote, is tolerant and civilized and "gives each boy a fair chance of developing his own individuality. The reason is perhaps that, being a very rich school, it can afford a large staff, which means that the masters are not overworked…" Crick, p. 101.

It is interesting that Orwell noted in his essay 'Why I Write" that he discovered the joy of mere words when he was sixteen but says nothing about Eton's influence on his thinking at the time. In another instance, in *The Road to Wigan Pier,* he refers to the fact that he went to "an expensive, snobbish school" but does not explicitly identify Eton.

In a way, Orwell seems to have bundled together all his school days in his reflections about St. Cyprian's. Whether correct or not, he looked back on that whole period as giving rise to a sense of failure:

"I had won two scholarships, but I was a failure, because success was measured not by what you did but by what you *were*. I was 'not a good type of boy' and could bring no credit on the school. I did not possess character or courage or health or strength or money, or even good manners, the power to look like a gentleman." CEJL Vol. 4, p. 363.

His parting with the headmaster and his wife of St. Cyprian's was awkward (note that his essay went unpublished until after Mrs. Wilkes had died in 1967):

"'Good-bye,' Flip's parting smile seemed to say; 'it's not worth quarreling now. You haven't made much of a success of your time at St. Cyprian's, have you? And I don't suppose you'll get on awfully well at a public school either. We made a mistake, really, in wasting our time and money on you…We know you disbelieve in everything we've taught you, and we know you aren't in the least grateful for all we've done for you. But there's no use in bringing it all up now. We aren't responsible for you any longer, and we shan't be seeing you again. Let's just admit that you're one of our failures and part without ill-feeling." CEJL Vol. 4, p.363-364.

*Such, Such Were The Joys* was published well after his death, but Orwell's essay had a huge effect in discussion about the ills and virtues of an English prep school (and to some extent about American prep schools such as Andover, Hotchkiss, Choate, etc.). Like many of his well-known novels and essays, *Such, Such Were The Joys* has lasted into our age whereas other school boy memoirs have faded from the scene. Even though Orwell has underplayed his time at St. Cyprian's, Wellington, and Eton, his school days nevertheless must have had a significant effect on his intellectual development. He was, after all, one of the most insightful, critical thinkers and prose stylists in the western world. For the time being, however, his departure from St. Cyprian's brought this thirteen-year-old some much needed relief:

"How happy I was, that winter morning, as the train bore me away with the gleaming new silk tie round my neck! The world was opening before me, just a little, like a grey sky which exhibits a crack of blue. A public school would be better fun than St. Cyprian's, but at bottom equally alien. In a world where the prime necessities were money, titled relatives, athleticism, tailor-made clothes, neatly-brushed hair, a charming smile, I was no good. All I gained was breathing-space." CEJL Vol. 4, p. 364.

# Burma

FOLLOWING HIS TIME AT ETON, ORWELL DID not go to university. His failure to do so was twofold. First, he had not performed well enough at Eton to win a scholarship. Second, his family could not afford to send him to university without one. It is one of those fortunate strokes of fate that George Orwell did not go to Oxford or Cambridge. Had he landed at either place, his literary career would have been entirely different, perhaps even non-existent. Orwell's unique approach to literature and politics was based upon an overall critique of the existing order, particularly British order. In addition, Orwell did not fit 'the mold' of a British university man. Orwell probably recognized this rebellious streak, but his tutor at Eton, Andrew Gow, definitely pegged Orwell as being unfit for university.

In 1921 Orwell's father, Richard Blair, went to Eton to talk with Gow about various career options for his son:

"Andrew Gow remembered Mr. Blair telling him that Eric could not go to Oxford without a scholarship; and that he told Mr. Blair that Eric did not stand the slightest chance of getting a scholarship—which settled the matter. And sixty years later Gow fumed that Eric would have brought disgrace on the College had they even put him forward for a scholarship examination, since he had done absolutely no work for five years… To have been to Eton at all was a good enough beginning for most careers. The idea of serving in India or Burma would have come up quite naturally and from the family, especially with his maternal grandmother still in Mandalay." Crick, p. 135-136.

Beginning in January 1922, Orwell spent six months cramming for the India Office's examinations. When he passed, he chose the Indian imperial police and listed his choices of where to be stationed in order: Burma, Bombay, Madras, and the Punjab. He was granted his first choice—Burma was not high on the list for desirable spots by British officials—and so the nineteen-year-old Orwell set sail for the sub-continent on 27 October 1922.

Perhaps it was well after his period of colonial service that Orwell had the time to think deeply that it was his family's lack of financial resources that paved the way to Burma and away from Oxford or Cambridge. Orwell could use his own experience to probe into the structure of British society. In fact, it was in his book, *The Road to Wigan Pier,* that Orwell gave the best sense of how Burma had changed his political outlook and sharpened his vision about the class system in British society:

"The Road from Mandalay to Wigan is a long one and the reasons for taking it are not immediately clear… I was born into what you might describe as the lower-upper-middle class. The upper-middle class, which had its heyday in the 'eighties and 'nineties, with Kipling as its poet laureate, was a sort of mound of wreckage left behind when the tide of Victorian prosperity receded. Or perhaps it would be better to change the metaphor and describe it not as a mound but as a layer—the layer of society lying between 2,000 pounds and 300 pounds a year; my own family was not far from the bottom. You notice that I define it in terms of money, because that is always the quickest way of making yourself understood. Nevertheless, the essential point about the English class-system is that it is *not* entirely explicable in terms of money. Roughly speaking it is a money-stratification, but it is also interpenetrated by a shadowy caste-system; rather like a jerry-built modern bungalow haunted by medieval ghosts." Wigan Pier, p. 121-122.

Ironically, Orwell discovered that Burma was free of that shadowy caste-system that plagued Britain. This was one of the few positive aspects of Burma he identified in both the quite mediocre novel he wrote to expunge his bad memories from there (*Burmese Days)* as well as in his later books. Again, *The Road to Wigan Pier*, of all his books, gives the most realistic accounts of his time in Burma. We quote the following at length from this book because this paragraph shines a light both on Orwell's thoughts on race and the caste-system, but also on another subject he could never seem to dismiss—the subject of smell:

"When I was not yet twenty I went to Burma, in the Indian Imperial Police. In an 'outpost of Empire' like Burma the class-question appeared at first sight to have been shelved. There was no obvious class-friction here, because the all-important thing was not whether you had been to one of the right schools but whether your skin was technically white. As a matter of fact, most of the white men in Burma were not of the type who in England would be called 'gentlemen,' but except for the common soldiers and a few nondescripts they lived lives appropriate to 'gentlemen'—had servants, that is, and called their evening meal 'dinner'—and officially they were regarded as being all of the same class. They were 'white men,' in contradistinction to the other and inferior class, the 'natives.' But one did not feel towards the 'natives' as one felt towards the 'lower classes' at home. The essential point was that the 'natives,' at any rate the Burmese, were not felt to be physically repulsive. One looked down on them as 'natives,' but one was quite ready to be physically intimate with them; and this, I noticed, was the case even with white men who had the most vicious color-prejudice. When you have a lot of servants you soon get into lazy habits, and I habitually allowed myself, for instance, to be dressed and undressed by my Burmese boy. This was because he was a Burman and undisgusting; I could not have endured to let an English manservant handle me in that intimate manner. I felt towards a Burman almost as I felt towards a woman. Like most other races, the Burmese have a distinctive smell—I cannot describe it: it is a smell that makes one's teeth tingle—but this smell never disgusted me. (Incidentally, Orientals say that *we* smell. The Chinese, I believe, say that a white man smells like a corpse. The Burmese say the same—though no Burman was ever rude enough to say so to me.)" Wigan Pier, p. 141-142.

In contrast to some of his positive comments about Burmans, Orwell discovers the unsuitable role of white men in that country, particularly the police force of which he was a part. In a telling passage early in Part II of The Road to Wigan Pier, Orwell points out that it took an American missionary to open his eyes to the futility of the British role in Burma:

"I remember once when I was inspecting a police station, an American missionary whom I knew fairly well came in for some purpose or other. Like most nonconformist missionaries he was a complete ass but quite a good fellow… One of my native sub-inspectors was bullying a suspect…The American watched it, and then turning to me said thoughtfully, 'I wouldn't care to have your job.' It made me horribly ashamed. So *that* was the kind of job I had! Even an ass of an American missionary, a teetotal cock-virgin from the Middle West, had the right to look down on me and pity me!" Wigan Pier, p. 145-146.

So begin Orwell's doubts about being a member of the Indian Imperial Police, but in addition to this, the passage contains a characteristic Orwell touch—a telling detail made fresh, prominent, and unexpected. It is this: "he was a complete ass but quite a good fellow." Seems an odd combination at first, but when one thinks about it perhaps there are indeed people one knows who fit this description. Orwell catches us, keeps us interested in the page being read.

He used another such detail in the essay he wrote relatively early on about a hanging he witnessed in Burma. The condemned man is being escorted to the gallows by two warders who grip him tightly by each shoulder. On his way there the prisoner steps to one side to avoid walking through a puddle in his path:

"It is curious, but till that moment I never realized what it means to destroy a healthy, conscious man. When I saw the prisoner step aside to avoid the puddle, I saw the mystery, the unspeakable wrongness, of cutting a life short when it is in full tide." CEJL Vol. I, p. 45.

A trivial thing, to avoid stepping into a puddle, but Orwell uses the detail effectively.

An even more remarkable essay arising from his time in Burma was perhaps Orwell's most famous: 'Shooting an Elephant.' Writing it a decade after leaving the country, Orwell had time to reflect on his philosophy about the British role in India and Burma and yet his essay was by no means a lecture to the British people nor was it a hard-hitting, sharp-elbowed editorial. Rather, Orwell's essay is a subtle inquiry into the nature of colonial rule based upon the unfolding of an unusual incident.

The language of the essay is plain, unadulterated, balanced. The opening is pure poetry:

"In Moulmein, in Lower Burma, I was hated by large numbers of people—the only time in my life that I have been important enough for this to happen to me."

Orwell then uses concrete examples in the same paragraph to describe the tension between the Burmese and their colonial masters:

"I was a sub-divisional police officer of the town, and in an aimless, petty kind of way anti-European feeling was very bitter. Not one had the guts to raise a riot, but if a European woman went through the bazaars alone somebody would probably spit betel juice over her dress. As a police officer, I was an obvious target and was baited whenever it seemed safe to do so. When a nimble Burman tripped me upon the football field and the referee (another Burman) looked the other way, the crowd yelled with hideous laughter…"

Finally, at the opening of the second paragraph, Orwell delivers his thesis, "…at the time I had already made up my mind that imperialism was an evil thing. " CEJL Vol. I, p. 235-236.

This way, Orwell takes an essay that is essentially a descriptive narrative but adds elements to it to make polemical without being overtly academic like a Mozart sonata which has a thread of melody one hardly notices. 'Shooting An Elephant' then has a thesis at the beginning, supporting examples within the body, and a masterful conclusion at the end.

As an Assistant District Superintendent police officer while in Moulmein, Orwell was summoned to deal with this rampaging elephant that had an attack of 'must' and had escaped from its master. Already the elephant had killed one man and might be quite dangerous. Orwell sends for an elephant rifle and is followed by a large group of Burmans:

"As soon as I saw the elephant I knew with perfect certainty that I ought not to shoot him. It is a serious matter to shoot a working elephant—it is comparable to destroying a huge and costly piece of machinery—and obviously one ought not to do it if it can possibly be avoided. And at that distance, peacefully eating, the elephant looked no more dangerous than a cow. I thought then and I think now that his attack of "must" was already passing off… But at that moment I glanced round at the crowd that had followed me. It was an immense crowd, two thousand at least and growing every minute.… They were watching me as they would watch a conjuror perform a trick. They did not like me, but with the magical rifle in my hands I was momentarily worth watching. And suddenly I realized I would have to shoot the elephant after all. The people expected it of me and I had got to do it; I could feel their two thousand wills pressing me forward, irresistibly. And it was at this moment, as I stood there with the rifle in my hands, that I first grasped the hollowness, the futility of the white man's dominion in the East… .I perceived in this moment that when the white man turns tyrant it is his own freedom that he destroys." CEJL Vol. I, p. 238-239.

At the time of this incident, Orwell was an obscure police official. He did not suddenly turn the event into a literary masterpiece while he was in Burma.

In fact, several of his contemporaries in Burma could hardly believe that Eric Blair and George Orwell were the same person.

"A more senior officer who visited him while in Twante found him 'tall, good looking, pleasant to talk to, easy of manner'; but he 'did not give the impression of being in any way remarkable'. Another found him a 'shy, diffident young man… obviously odd man out with other police officers but longing to, I think, to fit in.'" Crick, p. 153.

"'Much later, when I went back to Burma, I found that only a handful of people could recollect anything about him, and they remembered him merely as a sporting and skillful center-forward who scored many goals for the Moulmein police team. No one could quite believe that the author of 'Animal Farm' had been this man.'" Crick, p 166.

Burma would have been the tail end of Orwell's non-literary years. By the time he came to write 'Shooting An Elephant' a decade had passed since he had returned to Britain and in the mid-1930s he had hit his stride as a writer. He wrote the publisher John Lehmann in May 1936:

"What I was going to say was, I am writing a book at present & the only other thing I have in mind is a sketch, (it would be 2000-3000 words), describing the shooting of an elephant. It all came back to me very vividly the other day & and I would like to write it, but it may be that it is quite out of your line. I mean it might be too low brow for your paper…" CEJL Vol. I, p. 221. Lehmann went on to publish it in his magazine, *New Writing* and '*Shooting an Elephant*' has become one of the most widely anthologized essays in the English language.

Orwell concludes the essay with a masterful understatement:

"Afterwards of course there were endless discussions about the shooting of the elephant. The owner was furious, but he was only an Indian and could do nothing. Besides, legally I had done the right thing, for a mad elephant had to be killed, like a mad dog, if its owner fails to control it. Among the Europeans, opinion was divided. The older men said I was right, the younger men said it was a damn shame to shoot an elephant for killing a coolie, because an elephant was worth more than any damn Coringhee coolie. And afterwards I was very glad that the coolie had been killed; it put me legally in the right and it gave me sufficient pretext for shooting the elephant. I often wondered whether any of the others grasped that I had done it solely to avoid looking a fool." CEJL Vol. I, p. 242.

Following his posting in Moulmein, Orwell was sent to Katha in December 1926. The landscape was drier and more varied than the humid Delta postings to which he had been assigned earlier. Orwell used the surroundings of Katha in his novel *Burmese Days.* By then, he had made up his mind fully that British rule in India and Burma was a system from which he wanted to distance himself. Although he knew that the empire would certainly not change anytime soon, he could carry on his own private rebellion and begin to formulate his plan to leave. He describes in *The Road to Wigan Pier* how he was careful with whom he discussed his true feelings:

"I remember a night I spent on the train with a man in the Educational Service, a stranger to myself whose name I never discovered. It was too hot to sleep and we spent the night in talking. Half an hour's curious questioning decided each of us that the other was 'safe', and then for hours, while the train jolted slowly through the pitch black night, sitting up in our bunks with bottles of beer handy, we damned the British Empire—damned it from the inside, intelligently and intimately. It did us both good. But we had been speaking forbidden things, and in the haggard morning light as the train crawled into Mandalay, we parted as guilty as any adulterous couple." Wigan Pier, p. 145.

He resigned in 1927, bringing to an end 'five boring years within the sound of bugles.' Although Orwell was to write extensively about his attitude towards British imperialism and how this period had affected him as a writer and political thinker, he gave concise and simple answers to why he resigned:

"[B]ecause I disliked putting people in prison for the same things I should have done in the circumstances." (Orwell's own sentence). "I gave it up partly because the climate had ruined my health, partly because I already had vague ideas of writing books, but mainly because I could not go on any longer serving an imperialism which I had come to regard as very largely a racket." Crick, p. 171.

# Paris and London

George Orwell left Burma and returned to England in the late summer of 1927. Needless to say, his parents were not happy with his decision to leave his career in the colonial service and become a writer. He was different now: taller, thinner—his hair had grown dark—he sported a thin moustache and he smoked his cigarettes without much care to clear up the ashes (a habit from having a Burmese servant to clean up after him). He spent that fall with his family, and relations with his parents thawed. Determined to give his career as a writer a fresh start, he moved out that winter and through a friend found a cheap bedroom in which to live on Notting Hill. He wrote several short stories and sketches, none of which have survived. But he knew that his subject matter would be immersing himself with the poor, getting out of the respectable world altogether. As he wrote (looking back from 1936):

"When I came home on leave in 1927, I was already half determined to throw up my job, and one sniff of English air decided me. I was not going back to be a part of that evil despotism. But I wanted much more than merely to escape from my job. For five years, I had been part of an oppressive system, and it had left me with a bad conscience. Innumerable remembered faces—faces of prisoners in the dock, of men waiting in the condemned cells, of subordinates I had bullied and aged peasants I had snubbed, of servants and coolies I had hit with my fists in moments of rage… haunted me intolerably. I was conscious of an immense weight of guilt that I had got to expiate. I suppose that sounds exaggerated; but if you do a job for five years that you thoroughly disapprove of, you will probably feel the same." Wigan Pier, p. 147-148.

Having settled on his subject matter, Orwell finally set out one winter evening in shabby clothes he had picked up in a second-hand shop. He walked from Notting Hill to Limehouse Causeway until he found a common lodging-house that bore a sign 'Good Beds for Single Men.'

This was a sort of intelligence gathering venture. He saw a red-faced man lurching towards him but instead of a confrontation this fellow offered Orwell a 'baptismal' cup of tea. Later, he would feel confident enough to go out on the road and really get to know the underclass of British society.

It is interesting to note that in exploring London's East End, Orwell was following in the footsteps of an American writer he greatly admired: Jack London. In 1902 London explored the slums of the city and later wrote a book about his experiences called, *The People of the Abyss.* Orwell had read this work carefully while he was at Eton, and it obviously made a strong impression on him. Even the language from the book mirrors what Orwell would write. For example, consider the excerpt from London's book (first passage) and compare it to Orwell (second passage).

"No sooner was I out on the streets that I was impressed by the difference in status effected by my clothes. All civility vanished from the demeanor of the common people with whom I came into contact… .I had become one of them. My frayed and out-at-the elbow jacket was the badge and advertisement of my class, which was their class… I now shared with them a comradeship. The man in corduroy and dirty neckerchief no longer addressed me as 'sir' or 'governor'. It was 'mate' now—and a fine and hearty word with a tingle to it…" Crick, p.184.

"Dressed as I was, I was half afraid the police would arrest me as a vagabond, and I dared not speak to anyone, imagining that they must notice a disparity between my accent and my clothes (Later I discovered that this never happened). My new clothes had put me instantly into a new world. Everyone's demeanor seemed to have changed abruptly. I helped a hawker pick up a barrow that he had upset. 'Thanks, mate,' he said with a grin. No one had called me mate before in my life—it was the clothes that had done it." Down and Out, p. 129.

In the spring of 1928, Orwell left London for Paris to live in a new environment and learn the craft of writing. Nothing came easy for him. He wrote and wrote and wrote but only published a couple of pot-boiling articles for minor journals in Paris and London. He lived off savings from his job in Burma; writing seemed difficult for him. Very little is known about this period of his life:

"In the autumn of 1929, Blair ran out of money and was reduced to taking a job as a dishwasher for a few weeks in a fashionable hotel on the rue de Rivoli… .No one who knew him there can now be found and only one reminiscent letter survives from a friend of his Paris days. If occasionally he sat in the literary cafes of St-Germain-des-Pres, there is no sign that he sought the company of other writers, established or apprentice; and he must have lived, even before he became destitute, a very quiet, simple, and solitary life." Crick, p.186.

The novel he wrote of his days in Paris and in London among the poor was *Down and Out in Paris and London*. The book opens with his time in Paris and does not explain how the narrator came to live in a cheap hotel on the Rue du Coq d'Or and yet the writing in this book, originally published in 1933, is remarkable:

"It was a very narrow street—a ravine of tall, leprous houses, lurching towards one another in queer attitudes, as though they had all been frozen in the act of collapse. All the houses were hotels and packed to the tiles with lodgers, mostly Poles, Arabs and Italians. At the foot of the hotels were tiny *bistros*, where you could be drunk for the equivalent of a shilling. On Saturday nights about a third of the male population was drunk. There was fighting over women, and the Arab navies who lived in the cheapest hotels used to conduct mysterious feuds, and fight them out with chairs and occasionally revolvers. At night the policemen would only come through the street two together. It was a fairly rackety place. And yet amid the noise and dirt lived the usual respectable French shopkeepers, bakers and laundresses and the like, keeping to themselves and quietly piling up small fortunes. It was quite a representative Paris slum." Down and Out, p. 5-6.

Notable in this paragraph are characteristics of Orwell's best writing. For example, this metaphor is fresh and original, "as though they had all been frozen in the act of collapse." His details are concrete. It's not that the Arabs fought with one another; it's that they fought with chairs and occasionally with revolvers.

Orwell always found his best writing when he directly experienced the conditions of his subject matter. In Paris, while he still had money from his job in Burma, nothing much came from his literary efforts. But after eighteen months, he ran out of money and could then describe his experiences with energy and his signature sense of immediacy.

In these passages from *Down and Out in Paris and London* that describe at first what it was like to run critically low on money, note how Orwell brings vitality to his writing by focusing on concrete details:

"You discover, for instance, the secrecy attached to poverty. At a sudden stroke you have been reduced to an income of six francs a day. But of course you dare not admit it—you have got to pretend that you are living quite as usual. From the start it tangles you in a net of lies, and even with the lies you can hardly manage it. You stop sending clothes to the laundry, and the laundress catches you in the street and asks you why; you mumble something, and she, thinking you are sending the clothes elsewhere, is your enemy for life. The tobacconist keeps asking why you have cut down your smoking. There are letters you want to answer, and cannot, because stamps are too expensive… You have to buy rye bread instead of household bread, because the rye loaves, though dearer, are round and can be smuggled in your pockets. This wastes you a franc a day." Down and Out, p. 17.

"You go to the baker's to buy a pound of bread, and you wait while the girl cuts a pound for another customer. She is clumsy, and cuts more than a pound, and you have exactly a franc. When you think that you too might be asked to pay two sous extra, and would have to confess that you could not, you bolt in panic.

"You have strayed into a respectable quarter, and you see a prosperous friend coming. To avoid him you dodge into the nearest cafe. Once in the cafe you must buy something, so you spend your last fifty centimes on a glass of black coffee with a dead fly in it. One could multiply these disasters by the hundred." Down and Out, p. 18.

"Being inexperienced, I handled the money badly, and sometimes I went a day without food. When this happened, I used to sell a few of my clothes, smuggling them out of the hotel in small packets and taking them to a second-hand shop in the Rue de la Montagne St. Genevieve. The shopman was a red haired Jew, an extraordinarily disagreeable man, who used to fall into furious rages at the sight of a client. From his manner one could have supposed that we had done some injury to him." Down and Out, p. 19.

"Within certain limits, it is actually true that the less money you have, the less you worry. When you have a hundred francs in the world you are liable to the most craven panics. When you have only three francs you are quite indifferent; for three francs will feed you till tomorrow, and you cannot think further than that. You are bored, but you are not afraid. You think vaguely, 'I shall be starving in a day or two—shocking, isn't it?' And then the mind wanders to other topics. A bread and margarine diet does, to some extent, provide its own anodyne."

"And there is another feeling that is a great consolation in poverty. I believe everyone who has been hard up has experienced it. It is a feeling of relief, almost of pleasure, at knowing yourself at last genuinely down and out. You have talked so often of going to the dogs—and well, here are the dogs, and you have reached them, and you can stand it. It takes off a lot of anxiety." Down and Out, p. 20-21.

Fortunately, Orwell relieved this extreme poverty in the fall of 1929 by landing a job as a dishwasher for several weeks in a fancy hotel on the Rue de Rivoli. One can't be sure how long this job actually lasted, but his firsthand experience as a dishwasher in a Paris hotel made a deep impression on him and again gave his writing about this subject a transforming authenticity. The kitchen scenes he describes in the Paris sections of *Down and Out in Paris and London* are the best in the book. Orwell was always able to focus on the unusual, sordid detail. Note how he ends one of these sections with understatement:

"Jules and I missed the last Metro home and had to sleep on the floor of the restaurant. The first thing we saw in the morning were two large rats sitting on the kitchen table, eating from a ham that stood there. It seemed a bad omen, and I was surer than ever that the Auberge de Jehan Cottard would turn out a failure." Down and Out, p. 105.

Actually, the restaurant survived and some of the details Orwell reported caused offense to restaurant owners and restaurant patrons. He notes, for example, that Americans "seemed to know nothing about good food. They would stuff themselves with disgusting American 'cereals,' and eat marmalade at tea, and drink vermouth after dinner, and order a *poulet a lar reine* at a hundred francs and then souse it in Worcester sauce." Down and Out, p. 82-83.

As for Orwell reporting on the inner workings of a kitchen in an expensive French restaurant in 1929, nothing could beat his description of the preparation of a fancy steak by a head chef. The following passage is a remarkable piece of reportage and underscores why this particular book ranks alongside *The Road to Wigan Pier* and *Homage to Catalonia* as achieving the best of Orwell's polemic books.

"In the kitchen the dirt was worse. It is not a figure of speech, it is a mere statement of fact to say that a French cook will spit in the soup—that is, if he is not going to drink it himself. He is an artist, but his art is not cleanliness. To a certain extent he is forever dirty because he an artist, for food, to look smart, needs dirty treatment. When a steak, for instance, is brought up for the head cook's inspection, he does not handle it with a fork. He picks it up with his fingers and slaps it down, runs his thumb around the dish and licks it to taste the gravy, runs it around and licks again, then steps back and contemplates the piece of meat like an artist judging a picture, then presses it lovingly into place with his fat, pink fingers, every one of which he has licked a hundred times that morning. When he is satisfied, he takes a cloth and wipes his fingerprints from the dish, and hands it to the waiter. And the waiter, of course, dips *his* fingers into the gravy—his nasty, greasy fingers which he is forever running through his brilliantined hair. Whenever one pays more than, say, ten francs for a dish of meat in Paris, one may be certain that it has been fingered in this manner. In very cheap restaurants it is different; there, the same trouble is not taken over the food, and it is just forked out of the pan and flung onto a plate, without handling. Roughly speaking, the more one pays for food, the more sweat and spittle one is obliged to eat with it." Down and Out, p. 80.

Of the eighteen months Orwell spent in Paris in 1928 and 1929, he worked as a dishwasher for about ten weeks or so at the very end. Enough time to observe and understand the "underside" of Paris, particularly the scenes behind the kitchen doors of the Parisian restaurant scene. The work was enormously taxing even for Orwell who was in his twenties and who had been used to hard, unpleasant work in the equatorial humidity of Burma. He worked fifteen to seventeen hours a day, and had time away from work only for his meals and for a ride back on the metro to his hotel room where he simply collapsed from fatigue and usually slept in his clothes that were soaked with sweat. In spite of his difficulties, he never wrote with self pity (perhaps because he knew at some point he would be leaving) but he did evince empathy for his fellow working men and women who were 'stuck.'

"When one is overworked, it is a good cure for self-pity to think of the thousands of people in Paris restaurants who work such hours, and will go on doing it, not for a few weeks but for years. There was a girl in a *bistro* near my hotel who worked from seven in the morning till midnight for a whole year, only sitting down to her meals. I remember once asking her to come to a dance, and she laughed and said that she had not been further than the street corner for several months. But she was consumptive and died about the time I left Paris." Down and Out, p. 112.

Orwell finally left Paris in December 1929. He was absolutely exhausted and at the end of his rope. In the book, he says that he wrote a friend in London to borrow money to arrange his fare home and to see if he could find him a job (in real life Orwell probably got money to get home from his Aunt in Paris or from his family in England):

"After ten days I managed to find a free quarter of an hour, and wrote to my friend B. in London asking him if he could get me a job of some sort—anything, so long as it allowed more than five hours sleep. I was simply not equal to going one with a seventeen-hour day." Down and Out, p. 112.

Not long after, B. sent him a "fiver"—enough to get back to London and get his clothes out of pawn— and explained also that there was a job he could get for him. It was to look after a congenital imbecile. Orwell (as the narrator) was delighted:

"I pictured myself loafing in the country lanes, knocking thistle-heads off with my stick, feeding on roast lamb and treacle tart, and sleeping ten hours a night in sheets smelling of lavender." Down and Out, p. 115.

Alas, it was not to be. The narrator arrives in London but the congenital imbecile has been taken abroad for a month, and once again the narrator finds himself eventually penniless. This becomes the London section of the book. Orwell draws on his direct experiences as a tramp. His description of sleeping in a kip, or a common lodging house, is characteristically graphic. Six homeless men were already there sleeping on wood cots pushed together in a room fifteen feet square with an eight foot ceiling. The sheets were stained with sweat; his pillow a block of wood:

"Several noises recurred throughout the night. About once in an hour the man on my left—a sailor I think—woke up, swore vilely, and lighted a cigarette. Another man, a victim of a bladder disease, got up and noisily used the chamber-pot half a dozen times during the night. The man in the corner had a coughing fit once in every twenty minutes, so regularly that one came to listen for it as one listens for the next yap when a dog is baying at the moon. It was an unspeakable repellent sound; a foul bubbling and retching, as though the man's bowels were being churned up within him. Once when he struck a match I saw that he was a very old man, with a grey, sunken face like that of a corpse, and he was wearing his trousers wrapped around his head as a nightcap, a thing which for some reason disgusted me very much." Down and Out, p. 131.

Orwell had the direct experience of witnessing these sordid 'down and out' environments in London when he returned from Paris and would go out 'tramping.' Sometimes he would start out from his family home; most of the time he would be in London and would have stayed with friends. Often he was gone for weeks at a time. For a writer-journalist who had been raised in a comfortable 'lower upper middle class' environment, with his time at preparatory school and Eton—not to mention five years as a colonial police officer—his experience of going native in his own country was a real eye-opener. Consider this example of Orwell's description of an old age pensioner:

"I never realized that there are people in England who live on nothing but the old-age pension of ten shillings a week. None of these old men had any resources whatsoever. One of them was talkative, and I asked him how he managed to exist. He said:

'Well, there's ninepence a night for yer kip—that's five an' threepence a week. Then there's threepence on Saturday for a shave—that's five an' six. Then say you 'as a 'aircut once a month for sixpence—that's another threepence a week. So you 'as about four an' fourpence for food an' bacca.'

"He could imagine no other expenses. His food was bread and margarine and tea—towards the end of the week dry bread and tea without milk—and perhaps he got his clothes from charity. He seemed contented, valuing his bed and fire more than food. But, with an income of ten shillings a week, to spend money on a shave—it is awe-inspiring." Down and Out, p. 134.

Orwell also learned much from a fellow tramp named Paddy, an Irishman with whom he traveled for several weeks. "His features were good, but his cheeks had lanked and had that greyish, dirty in the grain look that comes from a bread and margarine diet." Down and Out, p. 149.

Paddy had been brought up in Ireland, served two years in the 1914-1918 war and then worked in a metal polish factory. By the time Orwell met him, Paddy had been unemployed for two years. "He was horribly ashamed of being a tramp, but he had picked up all the tramp's ways. He browsed the pavement unceasingly, never missing a cigarette end, or even an empty cigarette packet, as he used the tissue paper for rolling cigarettes." Down and Out, p. 150. Paddy always referred to foreigners as 'dem bloody dagoes' and because he had not been with a woman in years he was galvanized by the prospect of prostitutes rather than any respectable women. Orwell was surprised once when Paddy asked him whether Napoleon lived before Jesus Christ or after. Down and Out, p. 151.

*Down and Out in Paris and London*, then, becomes a kind of chronicle of the low life—not only does Orwell reveal the habits of tramps but also illuminates how they think and speak. As always, he is interested in language. Towards the end of the book he provides an interesting glossary of slang for British street life:

A gagger—beggar or street performer of any kind.
A moocher—one who begs outright, without pretense of doing a trade.
A nobbler—one who collects pennies for a beggar.
A chanter—a street singer.
A clodhopper—a street dancer.
A mugfaker—a street photographer.
A glimmer—one who watches vacant motor cars.
A gee (or jee—it is pronounced jee)—the accomplice of a cheapjack, who stimulates trade by pretending to buy something.
A split—a detective.
A flattie—a policeman.
A dideki—a gypsy.
A toby—a tramp.
A drop—money given to a beggar.
Funkum—lavender or other perfume sold in envelopes.
A boozer—a public house.
A slang—a hawker's license.
A kip—a place to sleep in or a night's lodging.
Smoke—London.
A judy—a woman.
The spike—the casual ward.
The lump—the casual ward.
A tosheroon—a half-crown.
A deaner—a shilling.
A hog—a shilling.
A sprowsie—a sixpence.

Clods—coppers.
A drum—a billy can.
Shackles—soup.
A chat—a louse.
Hard-up—tobacco made from cigarette ends.
A stick or a cane—a burglar's jemmy.
A peter—a safe.
A bly—a burglar's oxy-acetylene blow lamp.
To bawl—to suck or swallow.
To knock off—to steal.
To skipper—to sleep in the open.
Down and Out, 174-175.

The London sections of the book were added after Orwell finished the first draft in October 1930. He called it *A Scullion's Diary* and the book focused exclusively on his experiences in Paris. He submitted the manuscript to Jonathan Cape and was told that the work was too short and too fragmentary so he began work right away expanding it. After making these changes, adding some of the London material, he resubmitted the book to Cape but they turned it down again. Orwell then spent a good deal of time on another revision. Along with his tramping expeditions and work on his novel about Burma, he spent the better part of a year revising 'Down and Out'. He sent this new version to Faber and Faber. It took two months for Orwell to hear back. He received a letter from none other than T.S.Eliot, Faber's star literary man:

February 19th, 1932

Dear Mr. Blair:

I am sorry to have kept your manuscript. We did find it of very great interest, but I regret to say that it does not appear to me possible as a publishing venture. It is decidedly too short, and particularly for a book of such length it seems to me too loosely constructed, as the French and English episodes fall into two parts with very little to connect them. I should think, however, that you should have enough material from your experience to make a very interesting book on down-and-out life in England alone. With many thanks for letting me see the manuscript. I am yours faithfully,

T.S. Eliot

Discouraged, Orwell abandoned the manuscript with a new friend (of literary interests) named Mabel Fierz, telling her to destroy the manuscript but save the paper clips. Fortunately, she saw its merit and took the book to a good literary agent named Leonard Moore of Christy and Moore. Moore read the book and saw that it might be a good fit with a new, somewhat radical publishing firm headed by Victor Gollancz. In April 1932, Orwell wrote Moore:

Dear Mr. Moore:

Thank you for your letter... I left the ms you have with Mrs. Sinclair Fierz and asked her to throw it away, as I did not think it a good piece of work, but I suppose she sent it to you instead. I should of course be very pleased if you could sell it, and it is very kind of you to take the trouble of trying. No publishers have seen it except Faber's and Cape's. If by any chance you *do* get it accepted, will you please see that it is published pseudonymously, as I am not proud of it. CEJL Vol. I, p.77-78.

This appears to be the first time that Orwell expressed an interest in using a pseudonym for his published works. When indeed it turned out that Leonard Moore was successful in placing the book with Victor Gollancz, Orwell wrote: "I think if it is all the same to everybody I would prefer the book be published pseudonymously. I have no reputation that is lost by doing this and if the book has any kind of success I can always use the same pseudonym again." CEJL Vol. I, p. 85.

One of the readers at Gollancz, Gerald Gould, warned about the potential problems arising from obscenity, blasphemy and libel. Still, the book's unusual attributes outweighed this. Gould's report went on:

"This is an extraordinarily forceful and socially important document, and I think it most certainly ought to be published...I know nothing about the author but I am absolutely convinced of his genuineness. Nobody could have made up the experiences which he describes." Crick, p. 223.

By the time Orwell received the good news about his book he had accepted a job as headmaster at a boys school called The Hawthornes. His job as a teacher ran from April 1932 to December 1933. The entire student body was made up of 14 or 15 boys, ages 10 to 16. Although his job kept him busier than expected, his first priority was his writing. As such, he was more than happy to make changes to the manuscript that Gollancz recommended. Earlier, Gollancz had written to his solicitor, Harold Rubinstein, asking for his advice on changes to the book to help avoid legal problems. Orwell actually met with Gollancz and afterwards wrote Moore on 1 July 1932 about the meeting:

Dear Mr. Moore,

Thank you for your letter. I went & saw Mr. Gollancz at the time named, & he gave me a full account of the alterations he wants made in the book. Names are to be changed, swear words etc cut out… CEJL Vol. I, p. 84.

Orwell made the requested changes. Correcting the proofs took months. Gollancz wanted to publish the book during January 1934 and even though the finished proofs reached Orwell in November no one had made a firm decision on the title or the pseudonym. Gollancz wanted to use the title, 'The Confessions of a Down and Out' but Orwell wanted 'The Confessions of a Dishwasher' instead. As a compromise both agreed to the title, 'Down and Out in Paris and London.' As to the pseudonym, Orwell wrote his agent Moore on 19 November 1932:

Dear Mr. Moore,

Many thanks for your letter. I sent off the proof with the printer's queries on it yesterday. I made a few alterations and added one or two footnotes, but I think I arranged it so that there would be no need of "over-running". I will send on the other proof as soon as possible.

As to a pseudonym, a name I always use when tramping etc is P.S. Burton, but if you don't think this sounds a probable kind of name, what about

Kenneth Miles,
George Orwell,
H. Lewis Allways.
I rather favour George Orwell. CEJL Vol. I, p. 106.

So did everyone else involved. Thus was born one of the most famous pseudonyms in literature.

Following the publication of the British edition, a French edition of *Down and Out in Paris and London* was published in Paris in May 1935. On request, Orwell wrote an introduction to the French edition, which turned out to be unusually illuminating of the author. It follows:

"My kind translators have asked me to write a short preface for the French edition of this book. As probably many of my French readers will wonder, what chain of events brought me to Paris at the time when the incidents in this book took place, I think it would be best to begin by giving them a few biographical details.

"I was born in 1903. In 1922 I went to Burma where I joined the Indian Imperial Police. It was a job for which I was totally unsuited: so, at the beginning of 1928, while on leave in England, I gave in my resignation in the hopes of being able to earn my living by writing. I did just about as well at it as do many young people who take up a literary career—that is to say, not at all. My literary efforts in the first year barely brought me in twenty pounds.

"In the spring of 1928 I set off for Paris so as to live cheaply while writing two novels—which I regret to say were never published—and also to learn French. One of my Parisian friends found me a room in a cheap hotel in a working-class district which I have described briefly in the first chapter of this book, and which any sharp-witted Parisian will doubtless recognize. During the summer of 1929 I had written my two novels, which the publishers left on my hands, to find myself almost penniless and in urgent need of work. At the time it was not illegal—or at any rate not seriously illegal—for foreigners living in France to take jobs and it seemed more natural to me to stay in the city I was in, rather than return to England where, at that time, there were about two and a half million unemployed. So I stayed on in Paris and the events which I describe in this book took place towards the end of the autumn of 1929.

"As for the truth of my story, I think that I can say that I have exaggerated nothing in so far as all writers exaggerate by selecting. I did not feel that I had to describe events in the exact order in which they happened, but everything I have described did take place at one time or another… " CEJL Vol. I, p. 113-114.

This last point is enormously important. Because Orwell altered timelines of events (even though all events of which he wrote were accurate) he could not feasibly call this book non-fiction. Like *The Road To Wigan Pier*, this is best described as a documentary. There are also time-line alterations in *Homage to Catalonia* but Orwell never explicitly mentioned them as he did with this introduction to the French edition of *Down and Out in Paris and London.*

On the subject of Orwell's documentaries vs. outright novels, his biographer, Bernard Crick, makes a critical observation:

"Orwell had hoped that his first major publication would be a novel: he was in two minds whether *Down and Out* was journalism or literature. It was long before he realized that his documentaries were better than most of his novels." Crick, p. 225.

We could not agree more. To truly understand George Orwell, one has to focus, as we are here, on his documentaries and unfortunately gloss over his novels with the exceptions of course being *Animal Farm* and *1984.* So here is a brief account of Orwell's life between the publication of *Down and Out in Paris and London* and the commission he got to write *The Road to Wigan Pier.* He finished the first draft of *Burmese Days* by the summer of 1933. In September of that year he moved to Frayes College in Uxbridge, a larger and more respectable college than the Hawthornes which had run into financial difficulties. By December, he had retyped his revision of the novel. At some point during that month he caught pneumonia and was hospitalized. After he recovered, he gave up teaching and returned to his parents' home in Southwold. During this visit, he actually got along unusually well with his father, the two of them taking long walks together. In the meantime, having sent off *Burmese Days* to his agent, he began work on his next book, *A Clergyman's Daughter,* which he completed by November 1934. By then he had moved from Southwold to rooms above a bookshop in London called Booklovers' Corner where he could work with time to write during his off hours. Orwell's aunt, who lived in Paris, knew the owners of the bookshop quite well and helped secure him the job.

Orwell unfortunately did not earn much money working at the bookshop and had to try to borrow money from friends in the spring of 1935. By then, he was hard at work on his next novel called *Keep the Aspidistra Flying.* Towards the end of his life, Orwell essentially renounced both books as being substandard:

"Years later when Orwell was putting his affairs in order, he renounced both books. He left instructions that they were not to be translated or reprinted and "were written simply as an exercise" that he was desperate for money and that they should not have been published. Crick, p. 258-259.

Of the three books that Orwell wrote after *Down and Out,* he appreciated *Burmese Days* the most, although like the others it got mixed reviews. His friend from Eton, Cyril Connolly, reviewed the book for the *New Statesman and Nation:*

"*Burmese Days* is an admirable novel. It is a crisp, fierce, and almost boisterous attack on the Anglo-Indian. The author loves Burma, he goes to great lengths to describe the vices of the Burmese and the horror of the climate, but he loves it, and nothing can palliate, for him, the presence of a handful of inefficient complacent public school types who make their living there… His novel might have been better had he toned down the ferocious partiality of the Lawrence-Aldington school…" Crick, p. 265.

Two events soon changed Orwell's life for the better. In the summer of 1935 he met Eileen Maud O'Shaughnessy who would become his wife. In January 1936, Gollancz commissioned him to write a book about the conditions of the unemployed in the industrial north of England. Orwell was off to the races.

# Wigan Pier

ORWELL WOULD EXPAND GOLLANCZ'S PROPOSAL TO include employed coal miners as well as the unemployed. The advance of 500 pounds was significant—actually a little more than his father's yearly stipend—and even though it was to be spread over two years, it allowed Orwell to quit his job in the book shop and also to eventually marry Eileen. This advance also allowed him to become, for the first time, a professional writer.

He certainly fit the bill. During those months he was in the industrial north, Orwell worked tirelessly at staying in common homes, interviewing unemployed workers, going down mines (three times), attending political meetings, carefully typing up all his notes, and keeping a diary that survived in his papers. Called *The Road to Wigan Pier Diary* (31 January—25 March 1936). Orwell actually worked over the diary when done, never intending that it would be discarded. Its first entry is wonderfully characteristic of his eye for detail:

"31 January: To Coventry by train as arranged, arriving about 4 pm. Bed and Breakfast house, very lousy, 3/6d. Framed certificate in hall setting forth that (John Smith) had been elected to the rank of Primo Buffo. Two beds in a room—charge for room to yourself 5/-. Smell as in common lodging houses. Half-witted servant girl with a huge body, tiny head and rolls of fat at the back of neck curiously recalling ham-fat." CEJL Vol. 1, p. 170.

Orwell keeps track of the costs, inserts the detail about the framed certificate, mentions odor, and includes the image of the half-witted servant girl whose roll of fat on the back of her neck is like "ham-fat." Dense, concrete writing. When he toured up to Rudyard Lake that winter, he likewise wrote a diary entry containing remarkable imagery:

"3 February: Rudyard Lake (really a reservoir, supplying the potter towns) very depressing. In the summer it is a pleasure resort. Cafes, house-boats and pleasure-boats every ten yards, all deserted and fly-blown, this being the off-season. Notices related to fishing, but I examined the water and it did not look to me as though it had any fish in it. Not a soul anywhere and bitter wind blowing. All the broken ice had been blown up to the south end, and the waves were rocking it up and down, making a clank-clank, clank-clank—the most melancholy noise I have ever heard. (Mem. to use in a novel some time and to have an empty Craven A packet bobbing up and down among the ice)." CEJL Vol. 1, p. 171-172.

After staying in a bed and breakfast, as well as the home of the Meades, the husband of whom was a trade union official in Manchester, Orwell was directed by this couple to travel to Wigan. Here he stayed at a common lodging house on Warrington Lane but changed to another on Darlington Rd., which was a step down (perhaps that was Orwell's intention). This was the famous "tripe shop" with which Orwell opened his book. The diary entries for this place mirror many of the attributes listed in the final novel. Note below the comparison of the diary with the novel.

Diary

"15 February: They have found lodgings for me at Darlington Rd, over a tripe shop where they take in lodgers. The husband an ex-miner (age 58), the wife ill with a weak heart, in bed on sofa in kitchen. Social atmosphere much as at the previous place but house appreciably dirtier and very smelly...The family apart from the Fs themselves consists of a fat son who is at work somewhere and lives nearby, his wife Maggie who is in the shop nearly all day, their two kids, and Annie, fiancee of another son who is in London. Also, a daughter at Canada (Mrs. F says 'at Canada'). Maggie and Annie do practically the whole work of the house and shop. Annie very thin. overworked (she also works in a dress-sewing place) and obviously very unhappy. I gather that the marriage is by no means certain to take place but that Mrs. F treats Annie as a relative all the same and that Annie groans under her tyranny." CEJL Vol. 1, p. 178.

Novel

"The Brookers had large numbers of sons and daughters, most of whom had long since fled from the home. Some were in Canada—'at Canada,' as Mrs. Brooker used to put it. There was only one son living nearby, a large pig-like young man employed in a garage, who frequently came to the house for his meals. His wife was there all day with the two children, and most of the cooking and laundering was done by her and by Emmie, the fiancee of another son who was in London. Emmie was a fair-haired, sharp-nosed, unhappy looking girl who worked at one of the mills for some starvation wage, but nevertheless spent all her evenings in bondage at the Brookers' house. I gathered that the marriage was constantly being postponed and would probably never take place, but Mrs. Brooker had already appropriated Emmie as a daughter-in-law, and nagged her in that peculiar watchful, loving way that invalids have." Wigan Pier, p. 11-12.

Orwell's portrayal of Wigan endures not only because of the world-wide popularity of *Animal Farm* and *1984* but also because *The Road to Wigan Pier* broke new ground for its detail and 'camera-eye' journalism. As Orwell's biographer notes, the people of Wigan are justifiably touchy to this day about the tripe shop. Incidentally, tripe is an edible portion of the stomach lining from cows, pigs, or sheep.

Orwell often combined differing experiences into one—this was his novel writing technique rather than straight reportage. He was obviously fascinated by squalid details, dust on the furniture, fingerprints on the chamber pots, long-lasting bread crumbs on the kitchen table. He was fascinated by Mr. Brooker's dirty hands: "...like all people with permanently dirty hands he had a peculiarly intimate and lingering manner of handling things." Wigan Pier, p. 8. The tripe got special treatment:

"Even in the early morning when he [Mr. Brooker] descended into the mysterious den behind Mrs. Brooker's sofa and fished out the tripe, his hands were already black. I heard dreadful stories from the other lodgers about the place where the tripe was kept. Black beetles were said to swarm there. I do not know how often fresh consignments of tripe were ordered, but it was at long intervals, for Mrs. Brooker used to date events by it. 'Let me see now, I've had three lots of froze (frozen tripe) since that happened,' etc., etc. We lodgers were never given tripe to eat. At the time I imagined that this was because tripe was too expensive. I have since thought that this was because we knew too much about it. The Brookers never ate the tripe themselves, I noticed." Wigan Pier, p. 8.

When Bernard Crick's biography of Orwell appeared in 1980, he revealed interesting details about the famous Wigan tripe shop:

"There is no doubt that there *was* a tripe shop and that Orwell lodged there for about two weeks; also, that once the house was identified as 22 Darlington

Street (now Northcliff's Corsets') old people in the immediate neighborhood remembered it without prompting or hesitation, and confirmed the view of the present owner's mother that it had been a 'right filthy hole, a specially filthy hole.' (the long dead proprietors and their lodgers should not be named, but their names are to be found in the Wigan Burgess (voters) Lists for 1937 and are euphonious with Orwell's pseudonyms.)" Crick, p. 282.

As the train bore Orwell away from Wigan, he describes the memorable scene where from the train window he spots an impoverished woman trying to unclog an exterior drain pipe by poking a stick up into its foul contents. Orwell reflects that this young woman, who was probably twenty-five but looked closer to forty—knew precisely how awful her station in life was. In the trajectory of Orwell's career, these first books, particularly Down and Out and Wigan Pier, focused on the underside of life, the poor and lower working class. After he fought in the Spanish Civil War and reflected on the rise of the Soviet Union his last three books would demonstrate his ongoing battle with totalitarianism, but as he left Wigan on that train to travel to additional northern cities he was still preoccupied with the lower classes, and certainly most particularly with the lowest of the low:

His stay at the tripe shop made a deep impression on him:

"But it is no use saying that people like the Brookers are just disgusting and trying to put them out of mind. For they exist in tens and hundreds of thousands; they are one of the characteristic by-products of the modern world. You cannot disregard them if you accept the civilization that produced them. For this is part at least of what industrialism has done for us. Columbus sailed the Atlantic, the first steam engines tottered into motion, the British squares stood firm under the French guns at Waterloo, the one-eyed scoundrels of the nineteenth century praised God and filled their pockets: and this is where it all led—to labyrinthine slums and dark back kitchens with sickly, ageing people creeping round and round them like black beetles. It is a kind of duty to see and smell such places now and again, especially smell them, lest you forget that they exist; though perhaps it is better not to stay there too long." Wigan, p. 17.

Orwell had originally been commissioned to write a documentary report on the conditions of the unemployed in the North of England, but he actually spent more time reporting on active coal mines and coal miners for his book. The operation of a coal mine was particularly suited to Orwell's approach to writing—difficult, dirty work with unusual characteristics to describe. He mentions going down the cage elevator (3' x 8' for the floor, 6' high) to the pit bottom and then having to walk—actually stoop most of the way—to the coal face. Having to walk nearly a mile or more in a stooped fashion, because the gallery was often only five feet high or less in most places, was enormously difficult for Orwell who stood 6'-3." He often had to rest along the way. He describes the operation of the mine in detail: the loud coal extracting machine at the coal face, the rattle of the conveyor belt taking coal bins on tracks back to the pit bottom, the dust and darkness, rather like his vision of what hell would look like. He describes in detail the miners at work at the coal face, mostly on their knees with shovels and covered head to toe with coal dust so that they appeared as muscular iron statues. He was in awe at their strength and tenacity:

"It is only when you see the miners down the mine and naked that you realize what splendid men they are. Most of them are small (big men are at a disadvantage in that job) but nearly all of them have the most noble bodies; wide shoulders tapering to slender, supple waists, and small pronounced buttocks and sinewy thighs with not an ounce of waste flesh anywhere. In the hotter mines they wore only a pair of thin drawers, clogs, and knee pads; in the hottest mines of all only clogs and knee pads." Wigan Pier, p. 23.

Orwell wrote of the habits of the miners, what they ate on the job (cold tea, bread and dripping), their habits of washing their hands and faces, how it was bad luck to see your wife or any woman before going into mine. He described accidents where the roof of a mine gallery collapsed and killed or buried alive miners below. In one vignette he discussed how the elevator cage somehow did not properly slow down as it was lowering and all inside expected a terrible, deadly crash below. Even though the cage finally came down safely one of the miners had clenched his teeth so hard that he lost a tooth in the process. Orwell took page after page to describe the difficulties and hard work to extract coal:

"It may seem that I am exaggerating, though no one who has been down an old-fashioned pit (most of the pits in England are old-fashioned) and actually gone as far as the coal face, is likely to say so. But what I want to emphasize is this. Here is this frightful business of crawling to and fro, which to any normal person is a hard day's work in itself; and it is not part of the miner's work at all, it is merely an extra, like the City man's daily ride in the Tube. The miner does that journey to and fro, and sandwiched in between there are seven and a half hours of savage work.... This is the kind of point one is always liable to miss. When you think of a coal mine you think of depth, heat, darkness, blackened figures hacking at walls of coal; you don't think necessarily of those miles creeping to and fro." Wigan Pier, p. 29.

Towards the end of the first half of his book, Orwell inserts a curious quote—from a Manchester Guardian book review of one of his earlier books: "Set down in Wigan or Whitechapel Mr. Orwell would still exercise an unerring power of closing his vision to all that is good in order to proceed with his wholehearted vilification of humanity." Wigan Pier, p.74.

Orwell denied the charge, and yet the reviewer was spot on. Orwell almost always looked at the underside of the scene before him. In reporting on conditions in the industrial north of England, he avoided the good, dwelt on the bad. He describes the bad teeth and poor health of the inhabitants of Wigan. He points out the cramped conditions and terrible smells of the interiors, and of course mentions that the outdoor WC is often seventy yards away. He writes about the houses in Sheffield as having unwashed crockery in the sinks, filthy water in the bathtubs. In fact, he describes Sheffield as "the ugliest town in the Old World." Wigan Pier, p. 106. He discusses broken barrels being used as furniture and how inhabitants of new government housing would have to be deloused before occupying. Typical is the following:

"There are scenes that stand out vividly in my memory. The almost bare living room of a cottage in a little mining village, where the whole family was out of work and everyone seemed to be underfed; and the big family of grown-up sons and daughters sprawling aimlessly about, all strangely alike with red hair, splendid bones, and pinched faces ruined by malnutrition and idleness; and one tall son sitting by the fireplace, too listless even to notice the entry of a stranger, and slowly peeling a sticky sock from a bare foot. A dreadful room in Wigan where all the furniture seemed to be made of packing cases and barrel staves and was coming to pieces at that; and an old woman with a blackened neck and her hair coming down denouncing her landlord in a Lancashire-Irish accent; and her mother, aged well over ninety, sitting in the background on the barrel that served her as a commode and regarding us blankly with a yellow, cretinous face. I could fill up pages with memories of similar interiors." Wigan Pier, p. 59-60.

Near the beginning of the second half of *The Road to Wigan Pier,* Orwell provides a remarkable, and concise, explanation of why he became disenchanted with the rule of the British Empire and why, as a direct participant in that rule, he chose his unusual method for exorcising the guilt he felt for his years in Burma. The following explanation is important enough to requote:

"When I came home on leave in 1927, I was already half determined to throw up my job, and one sniff of English air decided me. I was not going back to be a part of that evil despotism. But I wanted much more than merely to escape from my job. For the five years I had been part of an oppressive system, and it had left me with a bad conscience… .I was conscious of an immense weight of guilt that I got to expiate. I suppose that sounds exaggerated; but if you do for five years a job that you thoroughly disapprove of, you will probably feel the same." Wigan Pier p. 147-148.

While he was in Burma, he began to plan meticulously how he would exorcise his guilt by immersing himself into the lives of the British working class. As one British writer said, Orwell "went native in his own country." He made detailed plans of dressing down into tramp's clothes, eating, sleeping, begging, and working (when there was work) as an English blue collar worker who was out of work:

"I felt that I had got to escape not merely from imperialism but from every form of man's dominion over man. I wanted to submerge myself, to get right down among the oppressed, to be one of them and on their side against their tyrants." Wigan Pier, p. 148.

When Orwell was living through his period of self-induced poverty, he had not yet developed his thoughts on socialism. "I had at that time no interest in Socialism or any other economic theory." Wigan Pier, p.149. And yet he uses the second half of *The Road to Wigan Pier* to explore in detail the very nature of socialism and socialists.

As noted by his publisher in the long introduction he chose to write for the book, Orwell "comes forward as a devil's advocate, and explains, with a great deal of sympathy, why, in his opinion, so many of the best people detest Socialism…" Wigan Pier, p. xi-xii.

This forward by Victor Gollancz provides a road map to the second half of the book. "Now the whole of this second part is highly provocative, not merely in his general argument, but also in detail after detail. I had in point of fact marked well over a hundred minor passages about which I thought I should like to argue with Mr. Orwell…" p. xii. Take the case of how Orwell compares socialists to cranks:

"One sometimes get the impression that the mere words 'Socialism' and 'Communism' draw towards them with magnetic force every fruit-juice drinker, nudist, sandal-wearer, sex-maniac, Quaker, 'Nature Cure' quack, pacifist and feminists in England." Wigan Pier, p. 174.

Gollancz took offense at Orwell's portrayal of vegetarians: "Even about vegetarians (I apologize to vegetarians for the 'even') Mr. Orwell is astray. The majority of vegetarians are vegetarians not because 'they want to add a few miserable years to their wretched lives' (I cannot find the exact passage at the moment but that is roughly what Mr. Orwell says), but because they find something disgusting in the consumption of dead flesh." p. xv.

What Orwell actually wrote was this:

"I have here a prospectus from another summer school which states its terms per week, and then asks me to say 'whether my diet is ordinary or vegetarian.' They take it for granted, you see, that it is necessary to ask this question. This kind of thing is by itself sufficient to alienate plenty of decent people. And their instinct is perfectly sound, for the food-crank is by definition a person willing to cut himself off from human society in hopes of adding five years on to the life of his carcass; that is, a person out of touch with common humanity." Wigan Pier, p.174-175.

Finally, Orwell concludes this 'socialists equal cranks" argument with a wonderful summing up:

"We have reached a stage when the very word 'Socialism' calls up, on the one hand, a picture of airplanes, tractors, and huge, glittering factories of glass and concrete; on the other, a picture of vegetarians with wilting beards, of Bolshevik commissars (half gangster, half gramophone), of earnest ladies in sandals, shock-headed Marxists chewing polysyllables, escaped Quakers, birth-control fanatics, and Labour Party backstairs-crawlers. Socialism, at least on this island, does not smell any longer of revolution and the overthrow of tyrants; it smells of crankishness, machine-worship, and the stupid cult of Russia." Wigan Pier, p. 216.

Orwell finished his research in March 1936 and returned to his home in Wallington to begin actual work on the book. Three notable events occurred during its composition. First, he got married to Eileen. Second, he wrote and published his remarkable essay 'Shooting An Elephant.' Third, he made a trip to Letchworth to attend a session of their summer school on socialism. From this trip he produced one of the more remarkable passages in *The Road To Wigan Pier:*

"One day this summer I was riding through Letchworth when the bus stopped and two dreadful-looking old men got on to it. They were both about sixty, both very short, pink and chubby, and both hatless. One of them was obscenely bald, the other had long grey hair bobbed in the Lloyd George style. They were dressed in pistachio-coloured shirts and khaki shorts into which their huge bottoms were crammed so tightly that you could study every dimple. Their appearance created a mild stir of horror on top of the bus. The man next to me, a commercial traveller I should say, glanced at me, at them, and back at me, and murmured, 'Socialists,' as who should say, 'Red Indians.'" Wigan Pier, p.174.

Note the unusual details that make this passage so memorable. "two dreadful-looking old men," both "short, pink, and chubby," one "obscenely bald," both dressed in "pistachio-coloured shirts and khaki shorts into which their huge bottoms were crammed so tightly that you could study every dimple." Their appearance created a "mild stir of horror" on and on and then the bit comparing these two to Red Indians from the Wild West. Just terrific.

When Orwell delivered the manuscript to Gollancz in the fall, the publisher wanted at first to print only the first section of the book. Orwell refused to cut it in half. And so Gollancz wrote his lengthy introduction to the book, endeavoring to modify or explain some of Orwell's sharp criticisms of socialism and socialists. Of course, he also praised the essential value of the book:

"We feel that a Foreword to *The Road to Wigan Pier* is desirable, not merely in view of the misconception to which I have referred, but also because we believe that the value of the book, for some members, can be greatly increased if just a hint is given of certain vital considerations that arise from a reading of it... . As to the positive value itself, no one of us has the smallest doubt. For myself, it has been a long time since I have read so *living* a book..." Wigan Pier, p. x-xi.

Orwell was no longer in Britain when the book was published. By then he had made up his mind to fight in the Spanish Civil War against Franco's forces. "This rise in fascism," he had said, "somebody's got to put a stop to it." With the support of his wife, he gathered together provisions (hawking the family silver to raise money) and left England for Spain at the end of 1936.

# Spain

ORWELL LEFT LONDON ON DECEMBER 22, 1936 and arrived in Barcelona on December 26th with a stop in Paris where he visited the American novelist, Henry Miller. By the time Orwell arrived in Spain, Barcelona was displaying the attributes of a modern city that had fully converted to socialism according to the revolutionary principles of the Republican side of the war. Orwell could not have been more in awe:

"It was the first time that I had ever been in a town where the working class was in the saddle." Catalonia, p. 4.

Buildings had been seized by the workers and were draped with red flags and had graffiti displaying the hammer and sickle. Churches were being demolished. Ceremonial forms of speech had disappeared; tipping was forbidden. There were no private motor cars (all had been commandeered) and the taxis and trams were painted red and black. Revolutionary posters were everywhere and loud speakers were bellowing revolutionary songs all day and well into the night.

"In outward appearance it was a town in which the wealthy classes had practically ceased to exist. Except for a small number of women and foreigners there were no 'well-dressed' people at all. Practically everyone wore rough working-class clothes, or blue overalls or some variant of the militia uniform. All this was queer and moving. There was much in it that I did not understand, in some ways I did not even like it, but I recognized it immediately as a state of affairs worth fighting for." Catalonia, p. 5.

Coupled with the excitement of revolution there was what Orwell described as an "evil atmosphere of war." Catalonia, p. 5. Roads and buildings were in disrepair. At night, the streets were poorly lit for fear of air-raids. Shops were half empty. Meat was scarce, milk unobtainable, and there were shortages of coal, sugar, gas, and bread. In fact, the lines for bread were often a hundred yards long. Nevertheless, the citizens were content and hopeful:

"Above all there was a belief in the revolution and the future, a feeling of having suddenly emerged into an era of equality and freedom. Human beings were trying to behave as human beings and not as cogs in the capitalist machine." Catalonia, p. 6.

Once Orwell arrived at the front, and with his usual reporter's eye, he was able to reveal details not often found in newspaper reports appearing back home or even memoirs written soon after the procession of events. For example, towards the beginning of the book, he delivers a 'mundane' portrait of the trenches at the front:

"In trench warfare five things are important: firewood, food, tobacco, candles and the enemy. In winter on the Zaragoza front they were important in that order, with the enemy a bad last. Except at night, when a surprise-attack was always conceivable, nobody bothered about the enemy. They were simply remote black insects whom one occasionally saw hopping to and fro. The real preoccupation of both armies was trying to keep warm." Catalonia, p. 23.

In addition to fighting off the cold (cold was a condition to which Orwell was particularly susceptible), there was also the issue of water:

"Our water, like our food, came on mule-back from Alcubierre, and each man's share worked out at about a quart a day. It was beastly water, hardly more transparent than milk. Theoretically it was for drinking only, but I always stole a pannikinful for washing in the mornings. I used to wash one day and shave the next; there was never enough water for both." Catalonia, p. 31.

And then of course Orwell never misses revealing details about smells and excrement:

"The position stank abominably, and outside the little enclosure of the barricade there was excrement everywhere. Some of the militiamen habitually defecated in the trench, a disgusting thing when one had to walk round it in the darkness." Catalonia, p. 31.

Finally in an echo from the pages of *All Quiet on the Western Front*, Orwell discusses the issues of sleeping and dirt:

"Dirt is a thing people make too much fuss about. It is astonishing how quickly you get used to doing without a handkerchief and to eating out of the tin pannikin in which you also wash. Nor was sleeping in one's clothes any hardship after a day or two. It was of course impossible to take one's clothes and especially one's boots off at night; one had to be ready to turn out instantly in case of an attack. In eighty nights I only took my clothes off three times, though

I did occasionally manage to get them off in the daytime. It was too cold for lice as yet, but rats and mice abounded. It is often said that you don't find rats and mice in the same place, but you do when there is enough food for them." Catalonia, p. 31-32.

If Orwell had listed 'the enemy' at the bottom of the list of items to worry about in trench warfare, the enemy soon came into play quite suddenly when Orwell's commanding officer ordered fifteen volunteers to storm an enemy parapet at night about 150 yards away.

These men crawled through a pasture of mud before getting to the first wire, cutting through that, and then to the second wire. Each man was given three grenades as well as extra ammunition for his rifle. Just as they cut through the second wire, a sentry in the enemy parapet opened fire. Then firing broke out on both sides. Lying on his stomach, Orwell had to shout to his comrades behind him to make sure to avoid shooting him in the back. When he threw his first grenade he saw that it exploded harmlessly in front of the parapet. He was in the midst of throwing his second grenade when his aim was disrupted by fire coming from the parapet and he never knew where this second grenade landed. However, when he threw his third grenade he saw that it landed inside the parapet, near the machine gun nest.

Now, it was time to charge the parapet but when the men got inside they found not a single fascist remaining. A few moments later, Orwell spotted an enemy soldier in the half-light of a hut behind the parapet and gave chase:

"He was bareheaded and seemed to have nothing on except a blanket which he was clutching round his shoulders. If I had fired I could have blown him to pieces. But for fear of shooting one another we had been ordered to use only bayonets once we were inside the parapet, and in any case I never even thought of firing. Instead, my mind leapt backward twenty years, to our boxing instructor at school, showing me in vivid pantomime how he had bayoneted a Turk at the Dardanelles. I gripped my rifle by the small of the butt and lunged at the man's back. He was just out of my reach. Another lunge: still out of reach. And for a little distance we proceeded like this, he rushing up the trench and I after him on the ground above, prodding at his shoulder-blades and never quite getting there—a comic memory for me to look back upon, though I suppose it seemed less comic to him." Catalonia, p. 92.

Here, Orwell has employed the memory of his boxing instructor to raise the description of the battle above the normal narrative to a near comic opera.

In turn, he makes the scene unique and memorable. How often are our daily lives interspersed with memory—there is a special quality to Orwell's writing that he would weave into the scene the boxing instructor from school days, who, we imagine, would have had an obvious delight to tell "war stories" to his young pupils.

The comic opera aspect of Orwell's actual fighting disappeared quickly in mid-June at 5:00 in the morning when Orwell was struck in the throat by a sniper's bullet. At the time, Orwell was talking to the sentries preparatory to changing the guard but made the mistake of standing where his head rose above the parapet and was framed by the morning sun behind him. He took the time to describe, in graphic, memorable terms, what it was like to be struck by a bullet:

"Roughly speaking it was the sensation of being *at the center* of an explosion. There seemed to be a loud bang and a blinding flash of light all around me, and I felt a tremendous shock—no pain, only a violent shock, such as you get from an electrical terminal; with it, a sense of utter weakness, a feeling of being stricken and shriveled up to nothing. The sand-bags in front of me receded into immense distance. I fancy you would feel much the same if you were struck by lightning. I knew immediately that I was hit, but because of the seeming bang and flash I thought it was a rifle nearby that had gone off accidentally and shot me. All this happened in a space of time much less than a second. The next moment my knees crumpled up and I was falling, my head hitting the ground with a violent bang which, to my relief, did not hurt. I had a numb, dazed feeling, a consciousness of being very badly hurt, but no pain in the ordinary sense." Catalonia, p. 185.

At this point, fellow soldiers gathered around him. One wanted to open his shirt. Orwell tried to ask where he'd been hit but found that he could hardly speak. Still, he was told he had been shot through the neck.

"I took it for granted that I was done for. I had never heard of a man or an animal getting a bullet through the middle of the neck and surviving it… There must have been about two minutes during which I assumed that I was killed. And that too was interesting—I mean it is interesting to know what your thoughts would be at such a time. My first thought, conventionally enough, was for my wife. My second was a violent resentment at having to leave this world which, when all is said and done, suits me so well. I had time to feel this very vividly." Catalonia, p. 186.

The men got Orwell onto a stretcher and carried him roughly for a mile and a half to an ambulance. The wounding had also damaged his right arm which had gone from a kind of paralysis to hurting damnably. As they marched along the tracks to the ambulance, "leaves of the silver poplars which, in places, fringed our trenches, brushed against my face; I thought what a good thing to be alive in a world where silver poplars grow. But all the while the pain in my arm was diabolical, making me swear and then try not to swear, because every time I breathed too hard the blood bubbled out of my mouth." Catalonia, p. 187.

He was taken to a hospital in a town called Sietamo where his wounds were tended to and where comrades appeared at his bedside and relieved him of all his personal possessions. That evening he was loaded onto an ambulance and taken on a difficult, bumpy ride. "It took me back to my early childhood and a dreadful thing called the Wiggle-Woggle at the White City Exhibition." Catalonia, p. 188. After a stop he was loaded onto a hospital train and sent to a hospital in Lerida. After a week he was sent to Barcelona. Finally, nine days after being hit, he had his wound examined by a competent surgeon.

"The doctor, a brisk, handsome man of about thirty, sat me down in a chair, grasped my tongue with a piece of rough gauze, pulled it out as far as it would go, thrust a dentist's mirror down my throat and told me to say 'Eh!' After doing this until my tongue was bleeding and my eyes running with water, he told me that one vocal chord was paralyzed.

"'When shall I get my voice back?' I said.

"Your voice? Oh, you'll never get your voice back,' he said cheerfully."

Fortunately, the doctor's diagnosis turned out wrong.

"For about two months I could not speak much above a whisper, but after that my voice became normal rather suddenly, the other vocal chord having 'compensated.' The pain in my arm was due to the bullet having pierced a bunch of nerves at the back of my neck...The wound was a curiosity in a small way and various doctors examined it with much clicking of tongues and "'Que suerte! Que suerte!' One of them told me with an air of authority that the bullet had missed the artery by about a millimeter. I don't know how he knew. No one I met at this time—doctors, nurses, or fellow patients—failed to assure that a man who is hit through the neck and survives it is the luckiest creature alive. I could not help thinking that it would have been even luckier not to be hit at all." Catalonia, p. 193-194.

Orwell made a slow recovery from his neck wound. Eventually discharged from the military on medical grounds, he returned to Barcelona on June 20, 1937. When he walked into the Hotel Continental, Eileen spotted him and rushed him back into the street so that she could explain the new circumstances to him:

"She told him that the police had begun a purge of Anarchists and POUM activists and their foreign supporters. The POUM had been declared illegal and the Anarchists had been disarmed by sudden raids. The news had been kept from the front for several days so that POUM units returning on leave were either disarmed and disbanded or arrested. Her own room had been searched by the police a few nights before…" Crick, p. 337.

Orwell now had to assimilate the stark contrast of fighting for the Spanish government, and risking his life, to prevent the rise of fascism on one hand and then finding himself a hunted man on the other.

"It was a queer situation that we were in. At night, one was a hunted fugitive, but in the daytime one could live an almost normal life. Every house known to harbor P.O.U.M. supporters was—or at any rate was likely to be—under observation and it was impossible to go to a hotel or boarding-house, because it had been decreed that on the arrival of a stranger the hotel-keeper must inform the police immediately. Practically this meant spending the night out of doors. In the daytime, in a town the size of Barcelona, you were fairly safe. The streets were thronged by Civil Guards, Assault Guards, Carabineros, and ordinary police, besides God knows how many spies in plain clothes; still, they could not stop everyone who passed, and if you looked normal you might escape notice." Catalonia, p. 215.

Both Orwell and his wife agreed that they needed to get out of Spain as quickly as possible and they were able to arrange passage to France with help from officials at the British Consul who drafted papers without it being known that Orwell had anything to do with the P.O.U.M. Fortunately Orwell escaped arrest:

"I had had five days of tiresome journeys, sleeping in impossible places, my arm was hurting damnably, and now these fools were chasing me to and fro and I had got to sleep on the ground again. That was about as far as my thoughts went. I did not make any of the correct political reflections. I never do when things are happening... Afterwards I can see the significance of events…" Catalonia, p. 212.

Orwell and Eileen crossed the frontier without incident. When the train stopped at a town in France he bought cigarettes and cigars and had tea with fresh milk. Returning to England, he set to work almost immediately on composing his book, but his instincts were correct that a sober, realistic analysis of the Spanish Civil War did not arise from his pen until he wrote his masterful essay called 'Looking Back on the Spanish Civil War' in the fall of 1942 which served as a blue-print for *1984*.

It took Orwell these four years to critically assess the Spanish Civil War. In this essay that was published in 1942, Orwell brought forth a thorough and balanced backward look at the conflict. While he was in Spain, he admitted that he did not have the sufficient perspective to add some of the most important aspects of the war into his book *Homage To Catalonia* (which sold a disappointing 700 some-odd copies when it was first printed).

During those four years after the war, he had time to think and assess and research the articles, pamphlets, and reporting that were written during and after the war. For the sake of history and in the context of the critical ideas that formed the basis of *Nineteen Eighty-Four*, the Spanish Civil War formed the starting point for Orwell's view of totalitarianism. He made this crystal clear in his essay which is both a review of the previous conflict as well as a blueprint for his last novel. As he wrote:

"I remember saying once to Arthur Koestler, 'History stopped in 1936,' at which he nodded in immediate understanding. We were both thinking of totalitarianism in general, but more particularly of the Spanish civil war. Early in life I had noticed that no event is ever correctly reported in a newspaper, but in Spain, for the first time, I saw newspaper reports which did not bear any relation to the facts, not even the relationship which is implied in an ordinary lie. I saw great battles reported where there had been no fighting, and complete silence where hundreds of men had been killed. I saw troops who had fought bravely denounced as cowards and traitors, and others who had never seen a shot fired hailed as the heroes of imaginary victories; and I saw newspapers in London retailing these lies and eager intellectuals building emotional superstructures over events that had never happened. I saw, in fact, history being written not in terms of what happened but of what ought to have happened according to various 'party lines.'" CEJL Vol. 2, p. 256-257.

To illustrate this point, Orwell mentions that the Nazis and fascists represented themselves as saving Spain from a Russian dictatorship and spreading the propaganda that there was a Russian army *inside* Spain during the conflict, numbering up to a half a million men.

"This kind of thing is frightening to me, because it often gives me the feeling that the very concept of objective truth is fading out of the world. After all, the chances are that those lies, or at any rate similar lies, will pass into history. How will the history of the Spanish war be written? If Franco remains in power his nominees will write the history books, and (to stick to my chosen point) that Russian army which never existed will become historical fact, and schoolchildren will learn about it generations hence." CEJL Vol. 2, p. 258.

Orwell admits that much of recorded history veers significantly from the truth, that it is inaccurate and biased, but the difference in the late 1930s was the abandonment of the idea that history *could* be truthfully written, that the actual facts could be discoverable.

"It is just this common basis of agreement, with its implication that human beings are all one species of animal, that totalitarianism destroys. Nazi theory indeed specifically denies that such a thing as 'the truth' exists. There is, for instance, no such thing as 'science.' There is only 'German science', 'Jewish science' etc. The implied objective of this line of thought is a nightmare world in which the Leader, or some ruling clique, controls not only the future but *the past.* If the Leader says of such and such an event, 'It never happened'—well, it never happened. If he says that two and two are five—well, two and two are five. This prospect frightens me much more than bombs—and after our experiences of the last few years that is not a frivolous statement." CEJL Vol. 2, p. 258-259.

Thus, as early as 1942, we see various ideas that would find their way into *Nineteen Eighty-Four* published six years later.

# World War Two

After Orwell and his wife returned to England from Spain, doctors discovered that he had a lesion on one of his lungs and strongly urged him to seek a warm climate for recuperation. An anonymous donor paid for the two of them to travel to Marrakesh. While there, Orwell made progress on a new novel called *Coming Up For Air,* a semi-autobiographical work in which the narrator, fearing the coming of war, decides to return to the scenes of happy childhood memories in lower Binfield. Orwell was able to complete the first draft of the book, but preparation for the coming war in England forced Orwell and his wife to return after six months.

In the spring of 1939 he delivered the finished manuscript to Victor Gollancz. Then in June of that year his father grew seriously ill and died of cancer on June 28th, his son at his side. *Coming up for Air* had been published that month and received good notices. The first 2000 copies sold out and another 1000 copies were printed and sold in a couple of years. The nostalgia for an innocent time described in the book changed harshly to the nightmare of war. As Orwell wrote later in an essay entitled, 'My Country Right Or Left:'

"For several years the coming of war was a nightmare to me, and at times I even made speeches and wrote pamphlets against it. But the night before the Russo-German pact was announced I dreamed that the war had started. It was one of those dreams which, whatever Freudian inner meanings they may have, do sometimes reveal to you the real state of your feelings. It taught me two things, first that I should be simply relieved when the long dreaded war started, secondly that I was patriotic at heart, would not sabotage or act against my own side, would support the war, would fight in it if at all possible. I came downstairs to find the newspaper announcing Ribbentrope's flight to Moscow. So war was coming, and the Government, even the Chamberlain Government, was assured of my loyalty." CEJL Vol. 1, p. 538-539.

Actually, Orwell's patriotism had always been somewhat complicated. On the one hand, he was deeply opposed to the British imperial rule in India and Burma. On the other hand, he was affectionate towards simple English customs—English tea, English gardens, standing at attention for the King:

"I grew up in an atmosphere tinged with militarism, and afterwards I spent five boring years within the sound of bugles. To this day it gives me a faint feeling of sacrilege not to stand to attention during "God Save The King." That is childish, of course, but I would sooner have had that kind of upbringing than be like the left-wing intellectuals who are so 'enlightened' that they cannot understand the most ordinary emotions." CEJL Vol. 1, p. 540.

When the war started in September 1939, Eileen went to live in London where she got a job at the Censorship Department for the government. She visited her husband in Wallington on the weekends. Orwell tried to enlist in the army, but was deemed medically unfit. He earned very little money from journalism. By mid-December he had finished his book of essays (published in March 1940) called *Inside the Whale*, which consisted of three rather long essays, the most notable of which was the essay called 'Charles Dickens.'

Because Orwell had been reading Dickens all his life (he said he was spoon-fed Dickens as a child), he was familiar in detail with most of his works. In fact, while he and Eileen were in Morocco, they requested to have mailed to them various copies of Dickens's novels which they had the time to read and discuss.

Orwell begins this essay with a discussion of Dickens's unusual diversity as a writer. Tagged as being a bourgeois writer, Dickens was also (as Orwell points out) a subversive writer, a radical writer, and one might say even a rebel. The substance of this essay is that Dickens made himself into an English institution even though he savagely attacked elements of English society:

"Yet he managed to [attack English institutions] without making himself hated, and more than this, the very people he attacked have swallowed him so completely that he has become a national institution himself. In its attitude towards Dickens the English public has always been a little like the elephant which feels a blow with a walking stick as a delightful tickling. Before I was ten years old I was having Dickens ladled down my throat by schoolmasters in whom even at that age I could see a strong resemblance to Mr. Creakle, and one knows without needing to be told that lawyers delight in Serjeant Buzfuz and that *Little Dorrit* is a favorite in the Home Office. Dickens seems to have succeeded in attacking everybody and offending nobody." CEJL Vol. 1, p. 415.

Orwell continues his essay with some special opinions about Dickens's approach to his singular craft of novel writing against the backdrop of Victorian England. Below is a series of Orwell's observations:

"If one examines his novels in detail one finds that his real subject-matter is the London commercial bourgeoisie and their hangers-on: lawyers, clerks, tradesmen, innkeepers, small craftsmen, and servants." CEJL Vol. 1, p. 415.

"The truth is that Dickens's criticism of society is almost exclusively moral... He attacks the law, parliamentary government, the educational systems and so forth, without ever clearly suggesting what he would put in their place." CEJL Vol. 1, p. 416.

"But Dickens is not a humbug, except in minor matters, and the strongest single impression one carries away from his books is that of a hatred of tyranny." CEJL Vol. 1, p. 427.

"At the back of his mind there is usually a half-belief that the whole apparatus of government is unnecessary. Parliament is simply Lord Coodle and Sir Thomas Doodle, the Empire is simply Major Bagstock and his Indian servant, the army is simply Colonel Chowser and Doctor Slammer, the public services are simply Bumble and the Circumlocution Office—and so on and so forth." CEJL Vol. 1, p. 430.

"Dickens's lack of vulgar nationalism is in part the mark of a real largeness of mind, and in part results from his negative, rather unhelpful political attitude. He is very much an Englishman, but he is hardly aware of it—certainly the thought of being an Englishman does not thrill him." CEJL Vol.1, p. 433.

"It is not merely a coincidence that Dickens never writes about agriculture and writes endlessly about food. He was a cockney, and London is the center of the earth in rather the same sense that the belly is the center of the body." CEJL Vol. 1, p. 441.

"Wonderfully as he can describe an *appearance*, Dickens does not often describe a *process*. The vivid pictures that he succeeds in leaving in one's memory are nearly always pictures of things seen in leisure moments, in the coffee rooms of country inns or through the windows of a stagecoach." CEJL Vol. 1, p.443.

Finally, Orwell provides an example of one of Dickens's signature characteristics as a writer. Noting that other Victorian writers sought to imitate Dickens and yet in one respect the "thing that cannot be imitated is his fertility of invention" particularly invoking turns of phrase and concreted details.

"The outstanding, unmistakable mark of Dickens's writing is the unnecessary detail." CEJL Vol. 1, p. 450. Orwell then gives a passage illustrating this:

(Jack Hopkins is relating a story at Bob Sawyer's party of a child who swallowed his sister's necklace).

"Next day the child swallowed two beads; the day after that he treated himself to three, and so on, till in a week's time he had got through the necklace—five and twenty beads in all. The sister, who was an industrious girl and seldom treated herself to a bit of finery, cried her eyes out at the loss of her necklace; looked high and low for it but I needn't say didn't find it. A few days afterwards, the family were at dinner—baked shoulder of mutton and potatoes under it—the child, who wasn't hungry, was playing about the room, when suddenly there was heard the devil of a noise, like a small hailstorm." CEJL Vol. 1, p. 450.

It turns out that the beads were ratting about the child's stomach cavity. But the unmistakable Dickens touch is the baked shoulder of mutton with potatoes under it. This detail does not advance the story. "It is something totally unnecessary, a florid little squiggle at the edge of the page; only, it is by just these squiggles that the special Dickens atmosphere is created." CEJL Vol. 1, p. 451. Like a wedding cake, Dickens's prose has everything piled on top of one another, detail on detail, embroidery on embroidery.

It is noteworthy that Orwell is most famous for his political vision that he elucidated in his two most popular novels, *Animal Farm a*nd *1984*, but in addition he was a remarkable literary critic with a keen eye for nuance and originality in other authors.

Orwell finally joined his wife in London in May 1940. To get work, he took a job as a theater critic for the publication *Time and Tide*. But he found the work rather dull and purposeless especially given the circumstances of the war. Sadly, the fighting hit home to the couple personally when they discovered that Eileen's brother had been killed in France during the troop evacuation from Dunkirk. It was rather ironic that her brother, Laurence O'Shaughnessy, was one of the best medical specialists in Britain for lung disease and could have been a huge help to his brother-in-law in the coming years had he lived.

At the beginning of summer, Orwell signed up for the newly formed Local Defense Volunteers which was later renamed the Home Guard. Now, "Sergeant Blair" could feel somewhat useful in preparing his recruits for a possible German invasion. Even though that invasion never materialized, the Germans began to bomb London indiscriminately in September of 1940, a period known as the Blitz. Orwell was unafraid of the bombs and would often walk through the streets to see the explosions, but at that time he was unduly pessimistic and had a jaded view of the future:

"Within two years, maybe a year, if only we can hang on, we shall see changes that will surprise the idiots who have no foresight. I daresay the London gutters will have to run with blood. All right, let them, if it is necessary. But when the red militias are billeted in the Ritz I shall still feel that the England I was taught to love so long ago and for such different reasons is somehow persisting." CEJL Vol. 1, p. 539-540.

If George Orwell had been killed in the Blitz of London, he would be remembered today as an important, but still relatively minor, British essayist and novelist in the same context as V.S. Pritchett, Cyril Connolly, Lytton Strachey, and Stephen Spender. These four were excellent writers (Strachey's book *Eminent Victorians* is itself a masterpiece) but none of them has achieved fame into the twenty-first century as Orwell has. None of them is a household name in the English speaking world whereas one hears 'Orwell' or 'Orwellian' almost every single day.

When asked at the beginning of the war to write a biographical entry for a reference book called Twentieth Century Authors, Orwell delivered a short, self-effacing, self-portrait which revealed wonderful details about his character:

"I served four months on the Aragon front with the P.O.U.M. militia, and was rather badly wounded, but luckily with no serious after-effects. Since that, except for spending a winter in Morocco, I cannot honestly say that I have done anything except write books and raise hens and vegetables.

"What I saw in Spain, and what I have seen since of the inner workings of left-wing political parties, have given me a horror of politics. I was for a while a member of the Independent Labor Party, but left them at the beginning of the present war because I considered that they were talking nonsense and proposing a line of policy that could only make it easier for Hitler. In sentiment I am definitely 'left', but I believe that a writer can only remain honest if he keeps free of party labels.The writers I care most about and never grow tired of are Shakespeare, Swift, Fielding, Dickens, Charles Reade, Samuel Butler, Zola, Flaubert, and, among modern writers, James Joyce, T.S. Eliot, and D.H. Lawrence. But I believe the modern writer who has influenced me the most is Somerset Maugham, whom I admire immensely for his power of telling a story straightforwardly and without frills. Outside my work the thing I care most about is gardening, especially vegetable gardening. I like English cookery and English beer, French red wines, Spanish white wines, Indian tea, strong tobacco, coal fires, candlelight, and comfortable chairs. I dislike big towns, noise, motor cars, the radio, tinned food, central heating, and 'modern' furniture. My wife's tastes fit in almost perfectly with my own. My health is wretched but it has never prevented me from doing anything that I wanted to, except, so far, fight in the present war. I ought perhaps to mention that though this account that I have given of myself is true, George Orwell is not my real name…" Crick, p. 410-411.

Orwell joined the Indian Section of the BBC as Empire "Talks" assistant on August 18, 1941 on a starting salary of 640 pounds a year, much larger than what he earned as a freelance writer. Orwell sought a greater contribution to the war effort and work at the BBC seemed the best way to do so given that he was in no physical condition to fight. He spent two weeks at Bedford College in Regent's Park on an induction course with other new recruits. He started formally on September 23 at Portland Place, the BBC's central London headquarters, and worked directly under Z.A. Bokhari who was in charge of the Indian Section. The top boss of the "Talks" section was, ironically enough, Guy Burgess, the spy who would later defect to the Soviet Union.

Much of Orwell's job was to provide academic and literary programs that would be presented over the air to listeners in India with the ultimate goal to help keep educated Indians sympathetic to the British cause in the war. Orwell invited T.S. Eliot, Dylan Thomas and E.M. Forster to give readings. He also wrote essays on Shakespeare, Oscar Wilde, George Bernard Shaw, and Jack London that others read over the air. Even though Orwell did many broadcasts himself, his voice was not suited for radio because of his throat injury. Sadly, none of the broadcasts Orwell made have survived.

Orwell's work as a propagandist was controversial. Fortunately, it taught him many lessons he would later use in *1984*. George Woodcock (a critic who later became a friend) wrote: "And now Comrade Orwell returns to his old imperialist allegiances and works at the BBC conducting British propaganda to fox the Indian masses…" To this, Orwell replied that he had no illusions but believed that he had "kept our propaganda slightly less disgusting than it might otherwise have been." Crick, p. 418.

On the personal front, Orwell's mother, Ida, moved to London in the summer of 1942 and took a job at the department store, Selfridge's, and his sister Avril also moved to London and took a job at a sheet metal factory. Orwell's wife Eileen transferred jobs to the Ministry of Food. The couple moved from Langford Court to a flat in Mortimer Crescent, Maida Vale. "If George and I didn't smoke so much," Eileen told a friend, "we'd be able to afford a better flat." Crick, p. 432.

Orwell's time working for the BBC provided him material for scenes he would write in *1984*. For example, the look of the main building on Portland Place was a model for Mini Truth. Also there was a perpetual smell of cabbage at the BBC Oxford Street staff canteen. In his war-time diary for 1942, Orwell wrote:

"The only time when one hears people singing in the BBC is in the early morning between 6 and 8. That is the time when the charwomen are at work. A huge army of them arrive all at the same time. They sit in the reception hall waiting for their brooms to be issued to them and making as much noise as a parrot house, and then they have wonderful choruses, all singing together as they sweep the passages. The place has a quite different atmosphere at this time from what it has later in the day." CEJL Vol. II, p. 430.

This image was transformed into the singing of the prole woman depicted in *1984.*

In September 1943, he wrote the Eastern Services Director a letter of resignation and made clear that he was resigning not because he disagreed with BBC policy or any kind of grievance but "because for some time past I have been conscious that I have been wasting my own time and the public money on doing work that produces no result." Crick, p. 421.

Orwell wanted to go back to the work of writing and journalism where he believed he could be more useful. Deep down he wanted to be a war correspondent but again his poor 'chest health' prevented this as a war correspondent would have to be attached to the Army and he simply could not pass a health exam. After various delays, he officially left the BBC on November 24, 1943.

Suddenly Orwell had extra time on his hands. He was offered a position as Literary Editor of *Tribune* but in the meantime he got started on a project he had been thinking about for some time. He began writing *Animal Farm.*

# Animal Farm

Orwell wrote *Animal Farm* during the winter of 1943-44 while he and Eileen were staying at their flat on Mortimer Crescent. Each evening he would read sections of the book to her and invite feedback. The next day, over coffee, she would share bits about the book with her friends who were working with her at the Ministry of Food.

Orwell had finally settled into a schedule that allowed time for writing this unique novel. In late November 1943, he resigned from the BBC, left the Home Guard and joined the left-wing publication *Tribune* where he worked three days a week as an editor and columnist.

Orwell's motivation for writing *Animal Farm* had been brewing for some time. In a preface he later wrote for the Ukrainian edition of the book, he explained:

"Up to 1939, and even later, the majority of English people were incapable of assessing the true nature of the Nazi regime in Germany, and now, with the Soviet regime, they are still to a large extent under the same sort of illusion.

"This has caused great harm to the Socialist movement in England, and had serious consequences for English foreign policy. Indeed in my opinion, nothing has contributed so much to the original idea of Socialism as the belief that Russia is a Socialist country and that every act of its rulers must be excused, if not imitated.

"And for the past ten years I have been convinced that the destruction of the Soviet myth was essential if we wanted a revival of the Socialist movement.

"On my return from Spain I thought of exposing the Soviet myth in a story that could be understood by almost anyone and which could be easily translated into other languages. However the actual details of the story did not come to me for some time until one day (I was then living in a small village) I saw a little boy, perhaps ten years old, driving a huge cart-horse along a narrow path, whipping it whenever it tried to turn. It struck me that if only such animals became aware of their strength we should have no power over them, and that men exploit animals in much the same way as the rich exploit the proletariat." CEJL Vol. 3, p. 405-406.

Orwell finished writing *Animal Farm* in February 1944. Right away, he knew he would have trouble getting it published. As he wrote to a friend that month, "I am writing a little squib which might amuse you when it comes out, but it is not so OK politically that I don't feel certain in advance that anyone will publish it. Perhaps that gives you a hint of its subject." CEJL Vol. 3, p. 95-96.

Its subject—under the surface of the animal stories—was of course a biting criticism of the Soviet Union and its leader, Joseph Stalin. At the time, the Soviets were wartime allies of Great Britain. Also, British intellectuals were naively in awe of the Soviet system of socialism. Orwell was justified to feel that his little book (masterpiece though it was) would have difficulty finding a publisher.

On March 19, 1944, Orwell sent the following letter to his regular publisher about *Animal Farm:*

"Dear Mr. Gollancz: I have just finished a book and the typing will be completed in a few days. You have the first refusal of my fiction books, and I think this comes under the heading of fiction. It is a little fairy story, about 30,000 words, with a political meaning. But I must tell you that it is—I think—completely unacceptable politically from your point of view (it is anti-Stalin)." Crick, p. 452.

Orwell wanted a quick answer from Gollancz on a decision to publish or not, and in early April Gollancz sent a note to Orwell, rejecting the book. He returned the typescript to Orwell's agent, Leonard Moore, with the following letter:

"My dear Moore: Here is the manuscript of *Animal Farm*, together with my note to Blair. I am highly critical of many aspects of internal and external Soviet policy: but I could not possibly publish (as Blair anticipated) a general attack of this nature." Crick, p. 454.

Having failed to secure publication of *Animal Farm* with his original publisher, Orwell next turned to several British publishers who—as the saying goes—slow-walked the manuscript. He also sent the book to publishers in America, one of whom was Dial Press. A letter he wrote about this to an American friend named Philip Rahv (who was co-founder of the *Partisan Review)* is quite revealing:

"I dare say the Dial people will have got my MS by about now. As you say you're in touch with them, I wonder if you could ask them to let you have a look at it. I think you'll agree that it deserves to be printed, but its 'message' is hardly a popular one nowadays. I am having hell and all to find a publisher for it here though normally I have no difficulty in publishing my stuff… A few weeks back a newspaper I write for regularly refused to print a book review of mine because it was anti-Stalinist in tone." CEJL Vol. 3, p. 141.

Orwell's agent Leonard Moore was shopping the book about and getting rejection after rejection. T.S. Eliot of the publishing firm, Faber and Faber, rejected the book on the grounds that it was an inopportune moment politically to publish such a work. The British publisher Jonathan Cape rejected it for essentially the same reason. Orwell's position vis-a-vis *Animal Farm* was complicated. As he wrote his agent:

"The real trouble is with Gollancz. The contract to bring him my next two novels is still extant, and as he has refused to regard *Animal Farm* as working off one of these, it looks as if he wants to keep to it. At the same time, I would prefer not to give or offer him any more books if we can get out of it. I have no quarrel with him personally, he has treated me generously and published my work when no one else would, but it is obviously unsatisfactory to be tied to a publisher who refuses or accepts books partly on political grounds and whose own political views are constantly changing. When I wrote *Animal Farm,* for instance, I knew in advance that it would be a very difficult book to find a publisher for, and having to submit it to Gollancz simply meant that much time wasted. This might happen over and over again, and judging by some of the things he has published in the last year or two, I doubt whether I could write anything that Gollancz would approve of. For example, I recently started a novel. Considering how much work I have to do elsewhere I don't expect to finish it till sometime in 1947, but I am pretty sure that Gollancz would refuse it when the time comes, unless by then his own views have altered again." CEJL Vol. 3, p. 392.

The novel to which Orwell referred in this letter was, of course, *1984*.

The repeated rejections of *Animal Farm* forced Orwell to the conclusion that he would have to publish the book himself as a two-shilling pamphlet via the Whitman Press which was a small operation run by a friend of his named Paul Potts. On July 18, 1944, he wrote his agent:

"Dear Mr. Moore: Thanks for your letter. ... Meanwhile could you send me the copy of the MS that you have. Faber replied in much the same manner as Cape's. Warburg again says he wants to see it & would publish it if he can see his way to getting the paper, but that is a big "if". If that falls through I am not going to tout it round further publishers, which wastes time & may lead to nothing, but shall publish it myself as a pamphlet at 2/-. I have already half-arranged to do so & and have got the necessary financial backing. With the demand for books there is now, and the strings I can pull in one or two papers, I have no doubt we should get our money back, though probably not make much profit..." CEJL Vol. 3, p. 186-187. (note: *Animal Farm* has sold in the millions)

It was then that Orwell wrote his lengthy preface to what would have been the self-published edition of *Animal Farm*. For decades, that preface had disappeared but then was discovered in 1972 among Orwell's papers. Titled, 'Freedom of the Press' the preface is devoted to the obvious censorship being employed by British publishers against books or pamphlets that were anti-Soviet and of course the obvious bent in favor of pro-Soviet material. "At this moment what is demanded by the prevailing orthodoxy is an uncritical admiration of Soviet Russia." Copyright: The Orwell Foundation.

Of course this preface also provided officials at the BBC the language to be etched onto Orwell's statue at the BBC building in London:

"If liberty means anything at all it means the right to tell people what they do not want to hear."

Orwell's efforts to get *Animal Farm* published was clouded by a personal tragedy. In February 1945, *The Observer* and *The Manchester Evening News* commissioned him to report on liberated Paris. By then Orwell and his wife had already adopted a son, Richard (of course a baby at the time), and when Orwell left for the continent, Eileen and Richard went to stay with her sister, Gwen O'Shaughnessy, at Stockton-on-Tees in County Durham.

Orwell met a number of writers while in Paris including P.G. Wodehouse, Malcolm Muggeridge, Andre Malraux, and Ernest Hemingway. In late March, Orwell went to Germany to accompany Allied forces on the march to Cologne. Unfortunately, he fell ill and was admitted into a hospital. In the meantime, Eileen had been sending urgent letters to his hotel in Paris. Tumors had been found on her uterus and she needed an emergency hysterectomy. When he returned to Paris, he found the batch of letters from her and telegraphed her, but by then she had died of cardiac arrest under anesthesia. She was only 39.

Orwell took military transport back to Britain and attended her funeral, but although stoic he was absolutely grief stricken. As he later wrote a friend:

"I lost my wife in March. I cannot remember whether you ever met her. It was a beastly, cruel business; however I don't think she expected to die (it happened during an operation), so perhaps it was not so bad as it might have been. I was in France at the time and only got back after she was dead. My little son is now 15 months. Fortunately, he has always had excellent health and I have got a very good nurse who looks after both him and me." CEJL Vol. 3, p. 400-401.

He returned back to Europe not long after the funeral. His visits to the defeated cities in Germany made a huge impression on him. "To walk through the ruined cities of Germany is to feel an actual doubt about the continuity of civilization."

The trip to Germany gave Orwell obvious ideas about the effect of a dictatorship in particular and of totalitarianism in general.

He was more determined than ever to get *Animal Farm* published. His loyalty to the publishing firm of Secker and Warburg brought about an inevitability that they would publish his book, not only because Fred Warburg saw that the book was a potential bestseller but also because he had an eye for Orwell's future books. He had already published *Homage to Catalonia.* Now it was just a question of acquiring the paper in 1945 to publish *Animal Farm.*

Orwell wrote Warburg on June 13, 1945:

"Dear Fred: I will send the blurb (for *Animal Farm)* as soon as possible. As to the contract for a novel I was in France when the two contracts reached me and I probably did not explain adequately why I did not sign the novel contract and struck out references to it in the other contract…" CEJL Vol. 3, p. 386.

Orwell then went on to explain that he had complications with his original publisher, Victor Gollancz, who had contractual rights to Orwell's next two novels. Even though Gollancz had rejected *Animal Farm*, he contended that that particular book 'did not count' as one of the two obligatory novels since it was so short and was more of a novella than a novel.

In July 1945, Orwell wrote his agent, Leonard Moore, about this very subject, referring to it as 'the other business.'

"Dear Mr. Moore: I had a talk with Warburg about the contract position. He is quite satisfied with my assurance that I will bring him all my future work, subject to the books of a special nature (e.g. that 'Britain in Pictures' book) being allowed to go elsewhere. He is not pressing for a hard and fast contract, but he would no doubt prefer to have one when the other business is settled." CEJL Vol. 3, p. 392.

*Animal Farm* was published on August 17, 1945. 4500 copies were printed and sold immediately. Two more months followed before Warburg could put out a second printing—this time, 10,000 copies. All sold out immediately. The book was an instant hit. Even though American publishers had turned the book down, a talent scout for Harcourt Brace had come to Britain to look for future prospects.

"It happened that Frank Morley, who had been with Faber before the War and had joined Harcourt Brace in New York, had come to Britain as soon as he could at the end of the War to see what readers were currently interested in. He asked to serve for a week or so in Bowes and Bowes, the Cambridge bookshop. On his first day there customers kept asking for a book that had sold out—the second impression of *Animal Farm*. He left the counter, read the single copy left in the postal orders' department, left for London and bought the American rights." Crick, p. 487.

Reaction to *Animal Farm* was enormously positive but also controversial. On one hand, the clarity of the prose and the unique telling of this group of animals who take on human characteristics charmed both young and old alike. On a deeper level, particularly in Britain, there was debate about Orwell's ultimate meaning. On one level, critics argued that Orwell meant his book as a polemic against socialism. On another level, most believed that Orwell intended his book to be an allegory about a socialist revolution betrayed.

Orwell's greatest concern was that, no matter what, the pigs (including *both* Stalin and Trotsky) had violated the first rule of animal equality by giving themselves extra rations. In a copy he gave to a friend, Orwell marked out what he described as the most important passage in the book:

"'Comrades!' he cried. 'You do not imagine, I hope, that we pigs are doing this in a spirit of selfishness and privilege? Many of us actually dislike milk and apples. I dislike them myself. Our sole object in taking these things is to preserve our health. Milk and apples (this has been proved by Science, comrades) contain substances absolutely necessary for the well being of a pig. We pigs are brain-workers. The whole management and organization of this farm depends on us. Day and night we are watching over your welfare. It is for *your* sake that we drink that milk and eat those apples. Do you know what would happen if we pigs failed in our duty? Jones would come back! Yes, Jones would come back! Surely comrades,' cried Squealer almost pleadingly, skipping from side to side and whisking his tail, 'surely there is no one among you who wants to see Jones come back.'" *Animal Farm*, p. 29.

Ultimately, the seven commandments of the revolution are abridged and reduced to the famous phrase: "All animals are equal, but some animals are more equal than others." *Animal Farm*, p. 90.

Orwell was not strict about his allegory. There are no firm answers about who the animals represent in the book, but generally, the symbolism in *Animal Farm* is agreed upon as follows:

The incompetent and ineffective Mr. Jones represents Czar Nicholas II. Napoleon represents Joseph Stalin. Snowball represents Leon Trotsky. Squealer represents Vyacheslav Molotov. Mollie represents the bourgeois middle class during the Russian Revolution.

When the proceeds started to come in from the book, Orwell could treat himself to a bit of social life. He would have lunch in Fleet Street with some of his literary friends such as Malcolm Muggeridge, Julian Symons and Anthony Powell. He would have high tea in Canonbury Square with old political friends such as Tosco Fyvel and Anthony Powell.

This is the Orwell one likes to remember, a settled, productive man unhampered by the constant demands of money and before he eventually shut himself off to write what would be his greatest book, *1984.*

# 1984

THE GENESIS OF *1984* BEGAN AS EARLY AS the Spanish Civil War in the mid-1930s when Orwell witnessed first-hand political abuses that would become some of the core principles of "the Party."

He first articulated these observations in his essay "Looking Back on the Spanish Civil War"—a critically important essay. Excerpts from this essay once again bear quoting at length:

"I remember saying once to Arthur Koestler, 'History stopped in 1936,' at which he nodded in immediate understanding. We were both thinking of totalitarianism in general, but more particularly of the Spanish civil war. Early in life I noticed that no event is ever correctly reported in a newspaper, but in Spain, for the first time, I saw newspaper reports that did not bear any relation to the facts, not even the relationship which is implied in an ordinary lie. I saw great battles reported where there had been no fighting, and complete silence where hundreds of men had been killed. I saw troops who had fought bravely denounced as cowards and traitors, and others who had never seen a shot fired hailed as the heroes of imaginary victories; and I saw newspapers retailing these lies and eager intellectuals building emotional superstructures over events that had never happened. I saw, in fact, history being written not in terms of what happened but of what ought to have happened, according to various 'party lines.'" CEJL Vol. 2, p. 256-257.

"This kind of thing is frightening to me, because it often gives me the feeling that the very concept of objective truth is fading out of the world. After all, the chances are that those lies, or at any rate similar lies, will pass into history. How will the history of the Spanish war be written? If Franco remains in power his nominees will write the history books and (to stick with my chosen point) that Russian army which never existed will become historical fact, and schoolchildren will learn about it generations hence." CEJL Vol. 2, p. 258.

"I know it is the fashion to say that most of recorded history is lies anyway. I am willing to believe that history is, for the most part, inaccurate and biased, but what is peculiar to our own age is the idea that history *could* be truthfully written. In the past people deliberately lied, or they unconsciously colored what they wrote, or they struggled after the truth, well knowing that they must make many mistakes; but in each case they discovered that 'the facts' existed and were more or less discoverable. And in practice there was always a considerable body of fact which would have been agreed to by almost everyone...It is just this common basis of agreement, with its implication that human beings are all of one species of animal, that totalitarianism destroys. Nazi theory indeed specifically denies that such a thing as 'the truth' exists. There is, for instance, no such thing as 'science.' There is only 'German science,' 'Jewish science' etc. The implied objective of this line of thought is a nightmare world in which the Leader, or some ruling clique, controls not only the future but *the past.* If the Leader says of such and such an event, 'It never happened'—well, it never happened. If he says that two and two are five—well two and two are five. This prospect frightens me much more than bombs." CEJL Vol. 2 p. 258-259.

At the time Orwell began work on *1984* he was living in Canonbury Square in London. Given that he focused on his work as well as devoting his time to his young son, he hired a live-in housekeeper named Susan Watson, aged 25. She later provided an unbiased account of Orwell's daily life that was summarized quite well by his biographer, Bernard Crick.

Orwell rose at around eight am, usually being tickled awake by his son, Richard. They would then have breakfast with strong tea. Watson remembered that Orwell would load twelve tablespoons of loose-leaf black tea into an enormous pot that one could barely lift when full. Then he would work until it was time to go out for lunch at one of the pubs nearby. This is the place where he would relax and enjoy exchanging literary and political talk over a beer and a sandwich.

In the afternoon he would pop into various second-hand shops, or come home to do some carpentry work. In the evening, he would oversee a 'high tea' in his household that featured good old-fashioned English food with scones etc. (he liked Yorkshire pudding on Sundays). After playing with Richard for a bit, he would begin work. He insisted on having a cup of hot Cadbury's chocolate precisely at ten pm that was served in a large Victorian Jubilee mug. He would then work until three am. Watson could hear the banging of his typewriter throughout the night.

"His clothes were famously casual. His wardrobe consisted of an 'awful pair of thick brown corduroy trousers,' a pair of thick grey flannel trousers, a 'rather nice' black corduroy jacket, a shaggy and battered old green-grey Harris tweed jacket, and 'best suit' of dark grey to black herringbone tweed of old-fashioned cut… He told Tosco Fyvel early in 1946 that he was fed up wearing old clothes and, now that he had a little money, would buy some new ones. But he never seems to have got round to doing so." Crick, p. 504.

In the spring of 1946, Orwell arranged to move members of his household to Jura, a small island off the Scottish coast. Before doing so, he wrote a series of journalist pieces, the most important of which was 'Politics and the English Language' which bears some scrutiny.

After pointing out that the decline of the English language is due ultimately to political and economic causes, Orwell mentions that, like an alcoholic who drinks because he believes his life to be a failure, "the slovenliness of our language makes it easier for us to have foolish thoughts." CEJL Vol. 4, p.128.

Orwell provides a list of poor writing habits. For example, meaningless words and 'dying metaphors' which are worn-out metaphors, not fresh or arresting, that have arrived to the point of cliche. Examples: toe the line, ride roughshod over, stand shoulder to shoulder with, play into the hands of, no axe to grind, grist to the mill, fishing in troubled waters, Achilles heel, swan song.

He also writes about pretentious diction: "Except for the useful abbreviations i.e., e.g., and etc., there is no real need for any of the hundreds of foreign phrases now current in English. Bad writers, and especially scientific, political, and sociological writers, are nearly always haunted by the notion that Latin or Greek words are grander than Saxon ones, and unnecessary words like *expedite, ameliorate, predict, extraneous, deracinated, clandestine, sub-aqueous* and hundreds of others constantly gain ground from their Anglo-Saxon opposite numbers." CEJL Vol. 4, p. 131.

Perhaps the most oft-quoted section of this essay was the bit where Orwell "translated" a section from the Bible into modern English:

"Now that I have made this catalogue of swindles and perversions, let me give another example of this kind of writing that they lead to. This time it must of its nature be an imaginary one. I am going to translate a passage of good English into modern English of the worst sort. Here is a well known verse from *Ecclesiastes:*

I returned, and saw under the sun, that the race is not to the swift, nor the battle to the strong, neither yet bread to the wise, nor yet riches to men of understanding, nor yet favor to men of skill; but time and chance happeneth to them all.

Here it is modern English:

Objective consideration of contemporary phenomena compels the conclusion that success or failure in competitive activities exhibits no tendency to be commensurate with innate capacity, but that a considerable element of the unpredictable must invariably be taken into account." CEJL Vol. 4, p.133.

After giving many examples of how certain political writing is bad writing, Orwell ends his essay with six rules for good writing:

i. Never use a metaphor, simile or other figure of speech which you are used to seeing it in print.
ii. Never use a long word where a short one will do.
iii. If it is possible to cut a word out, always cut it out.
iv. Never use the passive where you can use the active.
v. Never use a foreign phrase, a scientific word, or a jargon word if you can think of an everyday English equivalent.
vi. Break any of these rules sooner than saying anything outright barbarous. CEJL Vol. 4, p. 139.

The same month that Orwell published this essay, *Politics and the English Language,* (April 1946), he wrote a letter to A.S.F. Gow who had been his classical tutor when he was a student at Eton. Orwell's growing fame meant that he was hearing from members of his past. The letter provides a glimpse as to Orwell's outlook just prior to his departure to Jura:

"Dear Mr. Gow: It was very nice to hear from you after all this time… I am just at the point of dropping all journalism and other casual work for six months. I may start another book during that period, but I have resolved to stop hackwork for a bit, because I have been writing three articles a week for two years and for two years previous to that had been in the BBC where I wrote enough rubbish (news commentaries and so on) to fill a shelf of books. I have become more and more like a sucked orange and I am going to get out of it and go to Scotland for six months to a place where there is no telephone and not much of a postal service.

"A lot has happened to me since I saw you. I am very sorry to say I lost my wife a little over a year ago, very suddenly and unexpectedly although her health had been indifferent for some time. I have a little adopted son who is now nearly 2 and was about 10 months old when his mother, i.e. my wife, died. He was 3 weeks old when we adopted him. He is a splendid child and fortunately very healthy, and is a great pleasure to me…As you gathered I had a difficult time making a living out of writing at the start, though looking back now, and knowing what a racket literary journalism is, I see that I could have managed much better if I had known the ropes. At present the difficulty with all writers I know is that whereas it is quite easy to make a living by journalism and broadcasting, it is practically impossible to live by books. Before the war my wife and I used to live off my books, but then we lived in the country on five pounds a week, which you could do then, and we didn't have a child. The last few years life has been so ghastly expensive that I find the only way I can find to write books is to write long essays for the magazines and then reprint them. However all this hack work I have done in the last few years has had the advantage that it gets me a new public, and when I do publish a book it sells a lot more than mine used to before the war.

"About my name, I have used the name Orwell as a pen-name for a dozen years or more, and most of the people I know call me George, but I have never actually changed my name and some people still call me Blair. It is getting to be such a nuisance that I keep meaning to change it by deed poll, but you have to go to a solicitor etc which puts me off. Yours, Eric Blair

"PS. You couldn't be expected to read all the books your ex-pupils have produced, but I wonder whether you saw my last book but one, *Animal Farm*? If not, I'd be happy to send you a copy." CEJL Vol. 4, p.146-148.

All of Orwell's concern about lack of money, and needing to write 'hack-work' to make ends meet, would soon come to an end when the American publishers of *Animal Farm* produced a first print run of 50,000 copies and the Book-of-the-Month Club produced 540,000 copies for its September 1946 selection.

Orwell's planned trip to Jura was postponed yet again by the unexpected death of his older sister, Marjorie, from kidney disease on May 3, 1946. Finally, towards the end of the month, Orwell arrived on the island accompanied by his younger sister Avril. Later, they were joined by the housekeeper Susan Watson and her boyfriend, an ex-soldier and communist named David Holbrook who took a dislike to Orwell and found, after sneaking glances at his novel in progress, that he was wallowing in negativity and hopelessness. This assembly was joined by other writers and various guests to whom Orwell had extended invitations but they were not a happy group as a whole. Soon, Susan Watson and her boyfriend left the island as did some of the other guests.

In wintertime, Orwell wrote in an upstairs bedroom, mostly in bed while smoking cigarette after cigarette. In the summer he would write in a sitting room downstairs off the kitchen. Nevertheless, there was plenty to distract him, especially in summer. These activities included planting fruits and vegetables, shooting rabbits, tending to domestic geese, fishing for mackerel and trapping lobster.

When he returned with his group to Canonbury Square in London for part of the winter, he wrote one his friends:

"I haven't really done any work this summer—actually I have at last started my novel about the future, but I've only done about fifty pages and God knows when it will be finished. However it's something that is started which it wouldn't have been if I hadn't got away from regular journalism for a while. Soon I supposed I shall be back at it, but I am dropping some of it and am going to try to do mostly high-paid stuff which I needn't do so much of..." Crick, p. 517.

While he was in London, he set aside work on *1984* and produced several memorable essays among them was one called 'The Prevention of Literature.' This essay shows clearly that he was continuing to mull over the themes found in 1984. Below are excerpts that are good examples of this:

"The organized lying practiced by totalitarian states is not, as is sometimes claimed, a temporary expedient of the same nature as military deception. It is something integral to totalitarianism, something that would still continue even if concentration camps and secret police forces had ceased to be necessary."

"From the totalitarian point of view history is something to be created rather than learned. A totalitarian state is, in effect, a theocracy, and its ruling caste, in order to keep its position, has to be thought of as infallible."

"Totalitarianism demands, in fact, the continuous alteration of the past, and in the long run probably demands a disbelief in the very existence of objective truth. The friends of totalitarianism in this country usually tend to argue that since absolute truth is not attainable, a big lie is no worse than a little lie."

"Already there are countless people who would think it scandalous to falsify a scientific text-book, but would see nothing wrong in falsifying an historical fact." CEJL Vol. 4, p. 63-64.

While in London, Orwell was able to resume his old social schedule—pub lunches with friends, dinner guests, high teas, etc., even though it was one of the coldest winters on record. He also came to an agreement with his old publisher, Victor Gollancz, in which Gollancz released his contractual obligations on Orwell's next novels.

By April 1947 Orwell was back on Jura with Avril and Richard. He immediately continued work on *1984* at the end of May he could write to his publisher Warburg that he was about a third of the way through the book and hoped to have a first draft completed by October and the book completed in early 1948:

"I don't like talking about books before they are written, but I will tell you now that this is a novel about the future—that is, in a sense, a fantasy, but in the form of a naturalistic novel. That is what makes it a difficult job…" Crick, p. 525.

This was also the time that Orwell sent Warburg the long autobiographical essay 'Such, Such Were The Joys' about his school days at St. Cyprian's mentioned earlier in this book. Much has been discussed about thematic connections between this work and *1984*. Even though it is not known when Orwell wrote this essay, it *is* known that he had outlined *1984* as early as 1943 so it is possible he kept ideas from both works in his head at the same time.

On November 7, 1947, Orwell finished the first draft of *1984*. It was a heroic effort given that he was fighting a constant battle with his bad lungs. He often coughed up blood, especially in the night, and he was exhausted most of the time. He was reluctant to go into a hospital but finally agreed to do so and was admitted to an excellent facility called Hairmyres just outside of Glasgow. He was diagnosed with chronic fibrotic tuberculosis in both lungs with the left lung being more severely affected. By May of 1948, doctors allowed him to have his typewriter back even though he had to work from his hospital room. Finally, he was discharged from the hospital on July 28. Perhaps he could have extended his life if he had moved into a sanitorium then but he returned to Jura and rewrote *1984* line by line between August and November 1948.

Earlier he had written his friend George Woodcock that he wanted to stay on Jura primarily for his health but also because he would have fewer distractions for his writing:

"I can work here with fewer interruptions, and I think we shall be less cold here. The climate, although wet, is not quite so cold as England, and it is much easier to get fuel. We are saving our coal as much as possible and hope to start the winter with a reserve of three tons, and you can get oil by the 40-gallon drum here, whereas last winter in London you had to go down on your knees to get a gallon once a fortnight. Part of the winter may be pretty bleak and one is sometimes cut off from the mainland for a week or two, but it doesn't matter so long as you have flour to make scones." CEJL Vol. 4, p. 376.

The bit about the scones lends a peculiarly human touch to a man who was nearing the end of producing one of the great works of literature as well as nearing the end of his own life.

A problem for Orwell was that his manuscript was full of edits and marginalia. While he was in the hospital outside of Glasgow, he made copious notes and incorporated them into the typescript. These included modifications on Newspeak, Ingsoc, the Ministry of Truth, more observations about Oceania and Airstrip One, the role of O'Brien, the philosophy of Goldstein, the Appendix at the end of the book. There were certain scenes with Julia that were dropped. Others added.

All this came to an enormous issue as to who was to type the final draft. He explains this in a letter to his publisher, Fred Warburg:

"I shall finish the book early in November, and I am rather flinching from the job of typing it, because it is a very awkward thing to do in bed, where I still have to spend half the time. Also there will have to be carbon copies, a thing which always fidgets me, and the book is fearfully long. I should think well over 100,000 words, possibly 125,000. I can't send it away because it is an unbelievably bad MS and no one could make head or tail of it without explanation. On the other hand a skilled typist under my eye could do it easily enough. If you can think of anybody who would be willing to come, I will send money for the journey and full instructions. I think we could make her quite comfortable. There is always plenty to eat and I will see that she has a comfortable warm place to work in.

"I am not pleased with the book but I am not absolutely dissatisfied. I first thought of it in 1943. I think it is a good idea but the execution would have been better if I had not written it under the influence of TB. I haven't definitely fixed on the title but I am hesitating between "Nineteen Eighty-Four" and "The Last Man of Europe." CEJL Vol. 4, p. 448.

Orwell asked several others, in addition to his publisher, to provide a typist to type the final draft under his supervision. No one was able to come through. Labor was in short supply that winter. He could have attempted to make the journey to London but given how bad his health had deteriorated that really was not an option.

So he undertook the job himself. Half of the time, he would type in bed and half the time he would type at a table sitting on a kitchen chair. In addition to the top copy of the typescript he used two sets of carbons. The conditions in his bedroom were far from ideal for a man with lung problems. He increased his cigarette smoking. He also used a Valor paraffin-stove in bad repair to heat his room that smelled badly and gave off heavy fumes.

Finally, during the first week of December 1948, he finished his book and immediately posted it to Warburg. Orwell spent the remainder of the month in bed. Fred Warburg was astounded when he read through the manuscript and knew that not only did he have a tour de force on his hands with a huge upside but that he had to move fast on getting the book into print given Orwell's precarious health.

Warburg's partner, Roger Stenhouse, sent him a suggestion for a jacket blurb. Orwell's reply the day after Christmas is quite revealing, especially the bit about 'parodying the intellectual implications of totalitarianism':

"Dear Roger: Thanks so much for your letter. As to the blurb, I really don't think the approach in the draft you sent me is the right one. It makes the book sound as though it were a thriller mixed with a love story, & I didn't intend it to be primarily that. What it is really meant to do is to discuss the implications of dividing the world up into 'zones of influence' (I thought of it in 1944 as a result of the Tehran Conference), & in addition to indicate by parodying them the intellectual implications of totalitarianism. It has always seemed to me that people have not faced up to these & that , e.g. the persecution of scientists in Russia, is simply part of a logical process which should have been foreseeable 10-20 years ago." CEJL Vol. 4, p. 460.

Best here to review the highlights of the book. Note that it was published as *Nineteen Eighty-Four* in Britain and *1984* in the United States.

The novel opens with its protagonist, Winston Smith, returning home for his lunch break from his job as a low level employee in the Records Department of the Ministry of Truth. The opening sentence is iconic: "It was a bright cold day in April and the clocks were striking thirteen." As he ascends the seven flights of stairs to his dwelling in Victory Mansions he passes the giant posters on each landing which feature an enormous face. "It was one of those pictures which are so contrived that the eyes follow you about when you move. BIG BROTHER IS WATCHING YOU, the caption beneath it ran." 1984, p. 1.

Winston is living in London, chief city of Airstrip One, which is a province of Oceania. The world is divided into three huge nation states: Oceania, Eastasia, and Eurasia—at one time or another each of which is at war with one another. While in his flat, Winston is conscious of the telescreen there which could pick up most sounds and often visual images of him. "You had to live—did live, from habit that became instinct—in the assumption that every sound you made was overheard and, except in darkness, every movement scrutinized." 1984, p. 3.

As Winston gazes out the window, he looks at the enormous building which holds the Ministry of Truth and can just make out the elegant lettering on the building, the three slogans of the Party:

WAR IS PEACE

FREEDOM IS SLAVERY

IGNORANCE IS STRENGTH

In addition to the Ministry of Truth (which concerned itself with news, entertainment, education and the fine arts), there are three other ministries between which the entire apparatus of government was divided: the Ministry of Peace which concerned itself with war, the Ministry of Love, which maintained law and order; and the Ministry of Plenty which was responsible for economic affairs. "The Ministry of Love was the really frightening one. There were no windows in it at all. Winston had never been inside the Ministry of Love, nor within a half a kilometer of it. It was a place impossible to enter except on official business, and then only by penetrating through a maze of barbed-wire entanglements, steel doors, and hidden machine-gun nests. Even the streets leading up to its outer barriers were roamed by gorilla-faced guards in black uniforms, armed with jointed truncheons." 1984, p. 4-5.

While in his flat, Winston pulls from a desk drawer a diary and, while outside the view of the telescreen, writes down the date: "April 4th, 1984" his first entry. He is not sure even if it is 1984 or 1985 but he knows that he is in danger by writing in a diary. Winston decides to begin the diary on this particular day because of an incident which had happened that morning at the Ministry.

Winston remembers that morning's session of the Two Minutes Hate during which Party members gather and scream at a huge film clip of Emmanuel Goldstein, the supposed arch enemy of the Party and Big Brother. During this performance and while Party members are jumping up and down in their chairs, Winston takes note of two people there. The first is the dark haired girl from the fiction department who is about 27 and who later comes to play a critical role in the book. The other is a strongly built man named O'Brien who is a member of the Inner Party.

"Winston had seen O'Brien perhaps a dozen times in almost as many years. He felt deeply drawn to him and not solely because he was intrigued by the contrast between O'Brien's urbane manner and his prize fighter's physique. Much more it was because of a hope—that O'Brien's political orthodoxy was not perfect. Something in his face suggested it irresistibly. And again, perhaps it was not even unorthodoxy that was written in his face, but simply intelligence. But at any rate he had the appearance of being a person that you could talk to, if somehow you could cheat the telescreen and get him alone." 1984, p. 11.

In his flat, Winston contemplates his diary. Almost without thinking about it, he automatically writes:

Down With Big Brother
Down With Big Brother
Down With Big Brother

Over and over again so that he fills up nearly half a page. Suddenly a knock on the door forces him to panic that the Thought Police have discovered him already but this turns out only to be his neighbor, Mrs. Parsons, whose husband Tom works at the Ministry of Truth with Winston. She asks Winston to fix the drain in her sink. Winston sees the Parsons' children who playfully accuse him of treason against the Party. Mr. and Mrs. Parsons live in constant fear of being denounced by their own children.

Winston returns to his apartment. Trying to continue to write, he thinks of a dream he had seven years before during which a man who he is sure is O'Brien says to him, "We shall meet in the place where there is no darkness." By now, Winston has accepted that he will eventually be killed by the Thought Police. This acceptance heartens him. He comes to the realization that even if no one ever reads what he has written in his journal, "It was not by making yourself heard but by staying sane that you carried on the human heritage." 1984, p. 28.

Winston works in the Records Department of the Ministry of Truth correcting various 'errors' in past media. On the walls of his cubicle desk are three orifices and sitting on his desk is a machine called a speakwrite. One of the orifices was for written messages, another one was for newspapers, and a third was for disposal of waste paper into what was called a 'memory hole.' At the Ministry of Truth there were thousands and thousands of memory holes for documents due for destruction.

On this particular day, Winston has found four messages he has to deal with or sanitize. Here's a good example:

"The message he received referred to articles or news items which for one reason or another it was thought necessary to alter or, as the official phrase had it, to rectify. For example, it appeared from the Times of the seventeenth of March that Big Brother, in his speech on the previous day, had predicted that the South Indian front would remain quiet but that a Eurasian offensive would shortly be launched in North Africa. As it happened, the Eurasian Higher Command had launched its offensive in South India and left North Africa alone. It was therefore necessary to rewrite a paragraph of Big Brother's speech in such a way as to make him predict the thing that had actually happened." 1984, p. 39-40.

As soon as Winston is done rewriting what is expected for the various messages, he "clipped the speakwritten corrections to the appropriate copy of the Times and pushed them into the pneumatic tube." 1984, p. 40. Afterwards, he crumpled up the original messages and any excess paper and deposited them into the memory hole, presumably to be devoured by flames somewhere at the bottom of the building.

Winston's job is just one very tiny part of the Records Department in the overall structure of the Ministry of Truth. Thousands worked day by day and almost minute by minute to bring the past up to date. "History was being changed and in no case would it have been possible, once the deed was done, to prove that any falsification had taken place." 1984, p. 41. In fact, the largest section of the Record Department consisted simply of persons whose duty it was to track down and collect all copies of books, newspapers, and other documents which had been superseded and were due for destruction.

"A number of the Times which might, because of the changes in political alignment, or mistaken prophecies uttered by Big Brother, have been rewritten a dozen times still stood on the files bearing its original date, and no other copy existed to contradict it. Books, also, were recalled and rewritten again and again, and were invariably reissued without any admission that any alteration had been made." 1984, p. 41.

The Records Department was itself only a single branch of the Ministry of Truth whose primary job was "to supply the citizens of Oceania with newspapers, films, textbooks, telescreen programs, plays, novels—with every conceivable kind of information, instruction, or entertainment, from a statue to a slogan, from a lyric poem to a biological treatise, and from a child's spelling book to a Newspeak dictionary." 1984, p 44.

The mention of the Newspeak dictionary ties in with one of Winston's friends, Syme, a philologist who works in the Research Department and is helping to create the 11th edition of the Newspeak dictionary. Syme is an enthusiastic party member although Winston suspects that because of his intelligence and ability he would at some point be vaporized. Winston meets Syme for lunch in the canteen and has the standard meal on a metal tray of pinkish grey stew, a hunk of bread, a cube of cheese, a mug of milkless Victory Coffee, and one saccharine tablet. Each also has Victory Gin served in a small porcelain mug. Soon they are joined by Parsons, Winston's neighbor at Victory Mansions. Syme then begins to study a column of Newspeak words he's produced on a strip of paper while the two other men talk.

The concept of Newspeak is central to the themes in the novel. Orwell goes so far as to include an Appendix—The Principles of Newspeak—at the back of the book and references the Appendix as early as page 4.

The essential point of Newspeak is to narrow the English language to far fewer words than is being currently used. Eventually, Newspeak is to replace Oldspeak, which is the traditional language. Here are its essential characteristics:

"It was intended that when Newspeak had been adopted once and for all and Oldspeak forgotten, a heretical thought—that is a thought diverging from the principles of Ingsoc—should be literally unthinkable, at least so far as the thought is dependent on words. Its vocabulary was so constructed as to give exact and often very subtle expression to every meaning that a Party member could possibly wish to express, while excluding all other meanings and also the possibility of arriving at them by indirect methods. This was done partly by the invention of new words, but chiefly by eliminating the undesirable words and by stripping such words that remained of unorthodox meanings, and so far as possible of all secondary meanings whatever. To give a single example. The word free still existed in Newspeak, but it could only be used in such statements as 'This dog is free from lice' or 'This field is free from weeds.' It could not be used in its old sense of: 'politically free' or 'intellectually free' since political and intellectual freedom no longer existed even as concepts, and were therefore of necessity nameless. Quite apart from the suppression of definitely heretical words, reduction of vocabulary was regarded as an end in itself, and no word that could be dispensed with was allowed to survive. Newspeak was designed not to extend but to diminish the range of thought, and this purpose was indirectly assisted by cutting the choice of words down to a minimum." 1984, p. 310.

At the canteen, Syme delivers with much pride an explanation of the benefits of Newspeak:

"It's a beautiful thing, the destruction of words. Of course the great wastage is in the verbs and adjectives, but there are hundreds of nouns that can be got rid of as well. It isn't only the synonyms; there are also the antonyms. After all, what justification is there for a word which is simply the opposite of some other words? A word contains its opposite in itself. Take 'good' for instance. If you have a word like 'good' what need is there for a word like 'bad' 'Ungood' will do just as well—better because it is an exact opposite, which the other is not. Or again, if you want a stronger version of 'good' what sense is there in having a whole string of vague, senseless words like 'excellent' and 'splendid' and all the rest of them? 'Plusgood' covers the meaning, or 'doubleplusgood' if you want something stronger still." 1984 p. 52-53.

Syme detects a lack of enthusiasm on the part of Winston and says to him: "You don't grasp the beauty of the destruction of words." 1984, p. 53.

Syme's skepticism towards Winston is well founded. Throughout the novel, Winston is plagued with doubts about the propaganda of the Party. Moreover, deep in his bones, he feels that human society must have been better off in many ways before the Revolution. At the canteen, Winston looks around the room and sees the slovenly, poor conditions. "Had it always been like this? Had food always tasted like this?" 1984, p. 61.

He describes the canteen as a crowded, smelly place, with battered metal tables and chairs, and everything shoved so close together that the party members ended up rubbing elbows while they ate. About them is the pervasive smell of bad gin, bad coffee, the smell of dirty clothes and rotting stew. Orwell makes clear that what the citizens of Oceania are living through is far below the standards of what the Party had promised (as it was for the citizens of the Soviet Union and Germans during the war). Somehow things should have been better.

"Always in your stomach and in your skin there was a sort of protest, a feeling that you had been cheated of something that you had a right to. It was true that he had no memories of anything greatly different. In anytime that he could accurately remember, there had never been quite enough to eat, one had never had socks or under clothes that were not full of holes, furniture had always been battered and rickety, rooms underheated, tube trains crowded, houses falling to pieces, bread dark colored, tea a rarity, coffee filthy tasting, cigarettes insufficient—nothing cheap and plentiful except synthetic gin. And though, of course, it grew worse as one's body aged, was it not a sign that this was not the natural order of things, if one's heart sickened at the discomfort and dirt and scarcity, the interminable winters, the stickiness of one's socks, the lifts that never worked, the cold water, the gritty soap, the cigarettes that came to pieces, the food with its strange, evil tastes? Why should one feel it to be intolerable unless one had some kind of ancestral memory that things had once been different." 1984, p. 61.

Winston searches for further evidence of what life was like before the Revolution. To do so, he goes among the Proles. The social structure of Oceania is ranked from the highest, which are the Inner Party members, next are the Outer Party members, and finally at the low end of the scale, are the Proles, which are considered no better than cattle.

Winston goes into one of the pubs frequented by the Proles and takes up a conversation with an old man who he hopes would remember what life was like before the Revolution. Unfortunately the old man is confused and has a poor memory and cannot give Winston any useful information about the days before the Revolution.

The novel is hinged on Winston's deep skepticism about the utilitarian nature of Ingsoc (English Socialism). His is a discovery, unfortunately, of the worst of mankind in terms of governance.

The book progresses with Winston taking up with the dark haired girl from the fiction department, Julia, and what happens to them after they are discovered by the Thought Police. Here, O'Brien plays a principal role in laying bare the cruel elements of a true totalitarian state.

*1984* has sold millions and millions of copies and is one of the most important books in the English language. Unfortunately, by the time he finished his book and sent it off to be published, Orwell did not have much time to live.

Orwell left Jura for the last time on January 2nd 1949. Richard Reese accompanied Orwell on the train once he reached the mainland and they rode to Gloucestershire to a sanitorium called Cranham which stood 900 feet above sea level in the Cotswold Hills. It was a private facility. Each patient had a private chalet and was expected to take in the fresh air which was thought to be helpful for patients with lung disease. Orwell was strictly forbidden from using his typewriter so he wrote letters by hand, mostly to friends but also business/literary letters. In February he wrote a friend:

"My new book is a Utopia in the form of a novel. I ballsed it up rather, partly to being so ill while I was writing it, but I think some of the ideas in it might interest you. We haven't definitely fixed the title but I think it will be called 'Nineteen Eighty-Four.'" CEJL Vol. 4, p. 475.

In March he wrote Richard Reese:

"The doctor says I shall have to stay in bed for another two months—i.e. till about May—so I guess I won't actually be able to get out until about July… I don't mind being here. I am comfortable and well cared-for. I feel much better and my appetite is much better." CEJL Vol. 4, p. 479.

In spite of the care he was getting at Cranham, on the last day of March 1949 he wrote Richard Reese:

"I have been very poorly, spitting up large quantities of blood…There is evidently nothing very definite they can do for me. They talk of doing the 'thora' operation but the surgeon wouldn't undertake it because you have to have one sound lung which I haven't. Evidently the only thing to do is keep quiet. It worries me not to see Richard but perhaps later I can arrange for him to visit me. If I do get up this year I want to take him to a trip to London." CEJL Vol. 4, p. 487.

On May 16, he wrote his publisher, Frederick Warburg:

"Thanks much for your letter. I had to put Sonia Brownell off. I am in most ghastly health and have been for some weeks. I am due for another X-ray picture, but for some days I have been too feverish to go over to the X-ray room and stand up against the screen. When the picture is taken I am afraid there is not much doubt it will show that both lungs have deteriorated badly. I asked the doctor recently whether she thought I would survive and she wouldn't go further than saying she didn't know." CEJL Vol. 4, p. 500.

The mention of Sonia Brownell introduces a woman who would be Orwell's second wife even though he only had a few months to live. Twenty-nine years old at the time, Sonia had known Orwell for several years, having made the connection to him through Cyril Connolly's magazine *Horizon* where she worked. Even though she acquired the reputation of a gold digger, Sonia kept Orwell company and bore a sincere affection for him. When *1984* was published on June 8, 1949 in London by Secker & Warburg and in the US by Harcourt, Brace on June 13, 1949, Sonia worked tirelessly to promote the book.

When *1984* first appeared, it sold out the 25,500 copies that Warburg had printed. (A year after publication it had sold nearly 50,000 copies in Britain; 170,000 copies for Harcourt in the U.S. and 190,000 copies sold for the Book-of-the-Month Club selection.) The book created an immediate impression on both sides of the Atlantic, but Orwell was concerned that too many critics appeared to view his book as an attack on socialism and the Labor government of Britain. Even though Orwell made few public statements about his book, he took the time to write a revealing letter on June 16th to an official of the United Automobile Workers named Francis Henson who wanted to share the book with his members but was concerned that it was getting too much fanfare in the right wing press:

"My recent novel is NOT intended as an attack on Socialism or on the British Labor Party (of which I am a supporter) but as a show-up of the perversions to which a centralized economy is liable and which have already been partly realized in Communism and Fascism. I do not believe that the kind of society I described necessarily will arrive, but I believe (allowing for the fact that the book is a satire) that something resembling it could arrive. I also believe that totalitarian ideas have taken root in the minds of intellectuals everywhere, and I have tried to draw these ideas out to their logical consequences. The scene of the book is laid in Britain in order to emphasize that the English speaking races are not immediately better than anyone else and that totalitarianism, if not fought against, could triumph anywhere." CEJL Vol. 4, p. 502.

That summer, Orwell wrote his publisher:

"Dear Fred: Can you please send one copy each of *Burmese Days* and *Coming Up For Air* to Sonia Brownell, care of Horizon?

"I have Dr. Morland coming to see me again this evening. On and off I have been feeling absolutely ghastly. It comes and goes but I have periodical bouts of high temperatures etc. I will tell you what Morland says." CEJL Vol. 4, p. 505.

Morland was an expert in tuberculosis and what he said was that Orwell needed to be moved as soon as possible to University College Hospital London for better treatment. On September 3, 1948 he was transported by ambulance to UCH to a private room for which he paid seventeen pounds a week. Once settled he wrote to Warburg:

"As I warned you I might do, I intend getting married again (to Sonia) when I am once again in the land of the living, if I ever am. I feel ghastly and can't write much. We had a wonderful journey down yesterday in the most ritzy ambulance you can imagine. The beastly fever never goes away but is better some days than others… Morland says I mustn't see people much." Crick, p. 571-572.

Sonia took over managing many of his day to day activities, and she was very open to allowing Orwell's friends to come for short visits. Finally, his marriage took place on October 13th in a short ceremony in his hospital room. Orwell wore a red smoking jacket that had been given to him. Afterwards, David Astor treated the wedding party (absent the groom) to a fancy luncheon at the Ritz. Mutual friends said that Sonia and Orwell made love only one time. For her it was more an act of sympathy and yet they also said she truly loved him and was deeply anguished by his death.

In November, Dr. Morland recommended that Orwell move to a sanitorium in Switzerland where it was thought that the thin air would be easier on his lungs. Tuberculosis was often called consumption back in the 20th century and is caused by a bacterium (or germ) that has settled in the lung and begins to grow, often disintegrating the lining of the lung. What Morland feared most was that one of Orwell's lungs would have a major hemorrhage and that he would bleed to death or 'bleed out.'

During the last year of his life, Orwell kept a manuscript note-book in which he reflected on literary subjects. One of the entries is particularly telling:

"It is now 1949, sixteen years since my first book was published, and about 21 years since I started to publish articles in magazines. Throughout that time there has literally been not one day in which I did not feel that I was idling, that I was behind with the current job, and that my total output was miserably small. Even at the periods when I was working ten hours a day on a book, or turning out four or five articles a week, I have never been able to get away from this neurotic feeling that I was wasting my time. I can never get any sense of achievement out of the work that is actually in progress, because it always goes slower than I intend… ." CEJL Vol. 4, p. 510-511.

And yet the total of his quality writing would eventually be collected into twenty volumes. His ideas of political satire expressed in *Animal Farm* and *1984* would transcend the ages and have a larger impact on western society than anything written by his 20th century colleagues. Not a day passes where he is not mentioned in the western press with the words, Orwell or Orwellian. Many of his phrases have lasted into the twenty-first century such as "all animals are equal but some animals are more equal than others" or "Big Brother" or "Doublethink" or "Ingsoc, "Newspeak" or "The Ministry of Truth" or "The Thought Police, Memory Holes, Thought Crime," or "The Two Minutes Hate."

In a telling essay he wrote after *Animal Farm* was published called 'Why I Write' Orwell discussed his motivations as a political writer as well as the concept of a political conscience. He said that there were four motivations that compelled him to write a book: sheer egoism, aesthetic enthusiasm, historical impulse, political purpose:

"When I sit down to write a book, I do not say to myself, 'I am going to produce a work of art.' I write it because there is some lie that I want to expose, some fact to which I want to draw attention, and my initial concern is to get a hearing… So long as I remain alive and well I shall continue to feel strongly about prose style, to love the surface of the earth, to take pleasure in solid objects and scraps of useless information. It is no use trying to suppress that side of myself. The job is to reconcile my ingrained likes and dislikes with the essentially public, non-individual activities that this age forces on all of us.

"I cannot say with certainty which of my motives are the strongest, but I know which of them deserve to be followed. And looking back through my work, I see that it is invariably that I lacked a *political* purpose that I wrote lifeless books…" CEJL Vol. I, p. 6-7.

Even though his condition was worsening, plans to move him to Switzerland were still moving forward during the Christmas season. An air ambulance had been arranged for the end of January, but on the night of January 21, 1950 what Dr. Morland feared most happened. One of Orwell's lungs badly hemorrhaged, causing him to bleed out, and he died at once and alone before Sonia could be found. That morning, the BBC broadcast news of his death:

"The death occurred in London today of Mr. George Orwell, the author, at the age of 46. He had been ill for a long time. George Orwell was educated at Eton and later served in the Burma police. He fought on the Republican side in the Spanish Civil War and was wounded. After that he spent most of his time writing. He will, perhaps, be best remembered for *Animal Farm*, a satire on life in the Soviet Union, and for the recently published *Nineteen Eighty-Four*, a grim imaginary picture of totalitarian Great Britain some thirty years from now, which was highly praised by critics on both sides of the Atlantic." Crick, p. 579-580.

He was buried in a country churchyard of All Saints, Sutton Courtenay, near his family estate. His headstone bore his birth name Eric Arthur Blair. He had never taken the time to legally change his name to George Orwell.

“

# Bibliography

Crick, Bernard, *George Orwell: A Life,* (London): Secker & Warburg, 1980

Orwell, Sonia Brownell ed., *The Collected Essays, Journalism and Letters of George Orwell,* Four Volumes, (New York): Harcourt Brace Jovanovitch, 1968

Orwell, George, *Down and Out in Paris and London,* (London): Gollanscz, 1933

Orwell, George, *The Road to Wigan Pier,* (London): Gollanscz, 1937

Orwell, George, *Homage to Catalonia,* (London): Secker & Warburg, 1938

Orwell, George, *Animal Farm*, (London): Secker & Warburg, 1945

Orwell, George, *Nineteen Eighty-Four*, (London): Secker & Warburg, 1949

# Suggested Further Reading

*On Nineteen Eighty-Four: A Biography* by D. J. Taylor 2019

*Orwell: The Authorized Biography* by Michael Sheldon 1991

*Orwell's Ghosts: Wisdom and Warnings for the Twenty-First Century* by Laura Beers 2024

*The Ministry of Truth: The Biography of George Orwell's 1984* by Dorian Lynskey 2019

*Why Orwell Matters* by Christopher Hitchens 2002

# Cune Press

Cune Press was founded in 1994 to publish thoughtful writing of public importance. Its name is derived from cuneiform—the wedge-shaped script developed in the ancient Near East that transformed human communication and laid the groundwork for civilization itself.

Unlike earlier writing systems, cuneiform was simpler and more adaptable, allowing merchants, landowners, and scholars to become literate. Clay tablets marked with wedge-shaped symbols enabled wide collaboration in trade, governance, and cultural life.

Through cuneiform, scholarship flourished, art took form, and what historians define as the world's first civilization emerged. Even when the Phoenicians developed their sound-based alphabet, they expressed it in cuneiform, underscoring the script's enduring influence.

The founding vision of Cune Press is rooted in the democratization of learning—the belief that rarefied ideas should be drawn down from dusty pedestals and placed into the public sphere, where they can engage, challenge, and enrich everyday life.

Cune Press is guided by a deep conviction that ordinary people, when entrusted with the most precious gifts of civilization—ideas, literature, and knowledge—will give culture its necessary elasticity and depth, especially in times of rapid change.

Today, Cune Press operates as part of Salaam Cultural Museum, continuing its commitment to publishing work that fosters insight, cultural understanding, and public dialogue, while remaining true to its original mission: to make important ideas accessible and alive in the world.

# Books from Cune Press

| Aswat: Voices from a Small Planet (a series from Cune Press) | |
|---|---|
| Looking Both Ways | Pauline Kaldas |
| Stage Warriors | Sarah Imes Borden |
| Stories My Father Told Me | Helen Zughaib & Elia Zughaib |
| Girl Fighters | Carolyn Han |

| Syria Crossroads (a series from Cune Press) | |
|---|---|
| Leaving Syria | Bill Dienst & Madi Williamson |
| Visit the Old City of Aleppo | Khaldoun Fansa |
| Stories My Father Told Me | Helen Zughaib, Elia Zughai |
| Steel & Silk | Sami Moubayed |
| The Road from Damascus | Scott C. Davis |
| A Pen of Damascus Steel | Ali Ferzat |
| White Carnations | Musa Rahum Abbas |
| The Dusk Visitor | Musa al-Halool |

| Bridge Between the Cultures (a series from Cune Press) | |
|---|---|
| Empower a Refugee | Patricia Martin Holt |
| Muslims, Arabs & Arab Americans | Nawar Shora |
| Confessions of a Knight Errant | Gretchen McCullough |
| Apartheid Is a Crime | Mats Svensson |
| Curse of the Achille Lauro | Reem al-Nimer |
| Escape to Aswan | Amal Sedky Winter |
| Jinwar and Other Stories | Alex Poppe |
| Old Enough to Know | Alice Rothchild |
| Shahrazad's Gift | Gretchen McCullough |

WCW

| West Coast Writers | |
|---|---|
| Fluid | Lisa Teasley |
| The Other Side of the Wall | Richard Hardigan |
| Kivu | Frederic Hunter |
| Finding Melody Sullivan | Alice Rothchild |
| Afghanistan & Beyond | Linda Sartor |
| Joss, the Ambassador's Wife | Frederic Hunter |
| The Soldier, the Builder, & the Diplomat | Steven Schlesser |

Cune Press: www.cunepress.com | www.salaamculturalmuseum.org

# About the Author

*Author photo by Jeff Moon*

Steven Schlesser is an independent scholar and freelance writer based in Portland, Oregon. His first book, *The Soldier, The Builder, and The Diplomat: Custer, The Titanic, and World War One*, was reissued in a second edition with a new introduction in 2023. A graduate of Claremont McKenna College and Vermont Law School, Schlesser writes a monthly newsletter and works in the wood products industry, mostly with manufactured housing.

www.ingramcontent.com/pod-product-compliance
Lightning Source LLC
Chambersburg PA
CBHW050010040726
47599CB00014B/1308

* 9 7 8 1 9 5 1 0 8 2 9 9 4 *